D0445074

ψ PB

JAN 08 2000

3 X ¹¹/00 ✓¹⁰/01
5 X ⁶/02 ✓ ⁹/02
5 X ⁶/02 ✓ ⁷/03
9 X ⁶/05 ✓ ¹⁰/05
14 X ⁵/09 ✓ ⁴/10
14 X ⁹/10 ✓ ²/11
14 X 4/09 V 2/13

The Complete Guide to

Eldercare

The Complete Guide to

Eldercare

A.J. Lee and
Melanie Callender, Ph.D.

All inquiries should be addressed to:
Barron's Educational Series, Inc.
250 Wireless Boulevard
Hauppauge, New York 11788
http://www.barronseduc.com

International Standard Book No. 0-7641-0173-0

Library of Congress Catalog Card No. 97-52182

Library of Congress Cataloging-in-Publication Data
Jones-Lee, Anita.
    The complete guide to eldercare / Anita Jones-Lee and
Melanie Callender.
        p.   cm.
    Includes bibliographical references and index.
    ISBN 0-7641-0173-0
    1. Aged—Care—United States. 2. Aging parents—Care—
United States. 3. Caregivers—United States. I. Callender,
Melanie. II. Title.
HV1461.J65 1998
362.6—dc21   97-52182
                                                        CIP

Printed in the United States of America
9 8 7 6 5 4 3 2 1

About the Authors

A.J. Lee is an attorney and a graduate of Harvard University and Harvard Law School. She has previously authored other books published by Barron's Educational Series, Inc.

Melanie Callender, Ph.D. is a licensed psychologist who practices in Somerset, New Jersey. She is a board member and partner of PsychHealth, P.A., a group practice that specializes in providing psychological care to the chronically ill.

Acknowledgments

We are deeply indebted to the staff of Barron's, in particular to Mark Miele and Grace Freedson, for their belief in this project and for their encouragement. Thanks are due also to my family and friends for understanding the long hours away from shared pastimes. Special thanks to my co-author, Melanie Callender, for her patience and energy. This book is dedicated to Lucille Thompkins Glenn.

A.J. Lee

My love and thanks are offered to my entire family, for their support and encouragement. As with many of the tasks I have undertaken in my lifetime, I received unwavering support from D.E.C., whose help is deeply valued and appreciated. My sincere appreciation is also extended to S.M., who provided access to research materials, and who regularly voiced a belief in my ability to fit one more project into an already busy life. Many of my colleagues provided support and input, often in the form of thoughts or anecdotes about their own concerns for their elderly loved ones. I would also like to thank my co-author, A.J. Lee, and my editor, Mark Miele.

This book is dedicated to K., with love, as a reminder that dreams can become reality with vision, faith, knowledge and perseverance.

Melanie Callender

Contents

1

About This Book

Events and problems that can profoundly change our lives sometimes approach silently.

Remote from our immediate daily concerns, events and problems can be safely ignored as we busy ourselves with changing the baby, running to the fax machine, and waving goodbye to our child as she leaves for summer camp. Events and problems are on the periphery of consciousness and concern, a background noise pleasantly elsewhere, like the sound of a distant train.

Then one day, suddenly, they are here. They are upon us, sweeping through our lives, changing attitudes, changing patterns, changing everything.

Rock music, civil rights, feminism . . . eldercare.

Eldercare?

Yes, eldercare, and what that means to us emotionally, financially, legally, and socially will alter those lives touched by it as dramatically as marriage, divorce, or childbearing. Eldercare is starting to seize the national consciousness as Americans themselves age and find that their parents, because of improved health care and fitness, are also living longer.

Language, in some sense, is a radar picking up the concerns of our society by its slang. Over the past two decades, as the eldest of America's baby boomers—the group of us born between 1945 and 1965—have started to turn fifty, our vocabulary has become peppered with new words like "eldercare," "caregiver," and "Sandwich Generation." The concerns of aging, and of the elderly, have started to slowly, but profoundly, seize the national consciousness.

But even as they arrive, they come in undefined and poorly understood, arriving in a way that seems so sudden, and unannounced, catching us off-guard and unprepared. We have so many questions and so few answers.

What *is* eldercare? Who are caregivers? The Sandwich Generation? "Well-spouses?" And what does this have to do with you?

Most Americans put off thinking about retirement, aging, and related issues until they can no longer be ignored. We put off even *thinking* about these issues because it *makes* us feel worried and anxious. Somewhere deep inside we really believe that just thinking about an event can hasten its occurrence. We even blame ourselves if we think ill of someone and they later become ill—so convinced are we that our thinking powers can reach out and transform possibility into a negative reality. That's why we don't make wills. For goodness sake, don't think about it—it may come true. Well, if you are a baby boomer, as we are, you're busy putting off thinking about a lot of things: retirement, aging, investing, just to name a few. And that relief you feel is illusory and temporary because the aging of our own bodies and the aging of our parents is a distant train headed our way.

Eldercare is any care you provide to an elderly person for whom you feel responsible. For most of us, the person we'll give this type of care to will be our mother or father. But the recipient may be almost anyone in your family—a father-in-law, mother-in-law, an aunt, uncle, or an aging, ill, or disabled spouse. "Elderly" itself has become a slippery word in our language. Only a generation ago, it meant anyone older than sixty-five years old. Now, as baby boomers age, elderly has been redefined. According to recent surveys, most people believe that "elderly" now begins later in life, somewhere around seventy to seventy-five years old. Or as an old joke goes, "old" is always twenty years older than you are today. Within the category of those qualifying as "elderly," you'll now find the so-called "young old" (sixty-five to seventy years old), "old" (seventy to seventy-nine years old) and the "old old" or "senior old" (over eighty years old). There is no doubt that as baby boomers start to bump up against these categories they will discard these labels in favor of snappier, less-threatening, younger-sounding ones.

The concerns you must address in providing care to someone you love are the same, regardless of the age and identity of the recipient.

Our common struggle to provide loving, cost-effective care makes it necessary—or should we say convenient—to assemble in a book on "eldercare" all of the types of care we may have to give to many different loved ones of various ages. We recognize the narrowness of the term "eldercare" and encourage you to look beyond it, instead focusing on how this information can help you.

Our approach in writing this book was to use each chapter to focus on concerns raised in caring for the elderly and then to highlight in a section called "Tips" the special concerns raised when caring for spouses and other loved ones. The split works out to about 90 percent of the information relating to providing care to the aged and 10 percent giving you tips on how providing care for other loved ones might differ from providing care to elderly loved ones. We think this approach will match the reality you are likely to face.

America _is_ aging, and the aging of America has produced not only a new language to describe ourselves and our parents as we age, but a whole new set of industries and professions that cater to the aged. Geriatricians (doctors who specialize in treating diseases and conditions of the elderly), attorneys specializing in elder law, senior residences for the independent and semi-independent elderly, and the American Association of Retired Persons (AARP) are just a few of the professions and groups that have mushroomed to serve the elderly.

In this book, when we use the word "caregiver" we mean people who provide any form of unpaid eldercare to family members or friends. For example, Louise Gottlieb is a typical baby boomer who became a caregiver without warning. One Saturday morning, Louise, a high school music teacher in upstate New York, got a phone call that changed her life. Her sixty-five-year-old mother Alice had been found wandering through the aisles of a grocery store unable to recall where she lived or who she was. "I never had a clue this was coming at me," Louise says. After settling her confused mother—once an active, vital woman who enjoyed rollerblading in Central Park—into the extra bedroom her college-age son had just vacated, Louise sat across the kitchen table staring at her husband of twenty-five years, numbed by the sudden multiplication of financial and emotional issues that had come crashing down on her household.

Louise is not unique. Studies show that six of every ten people can look forward to the day when they will be "sandwiched" between the financial crunches of financing college costs and financing care for one or more elderly parents. Nursing home costs can range from $30,000 to $100,000 annually. Home care can cost more than $500 a week. Even minimal care such as that provided by adult day-care centers for seniors can cost $40 to $80 a day. Where does the money come from? Are there any sources to help?

Here's the good news. Help is available. There *are* strategies to manage the costs of eldercare. This book will identify and explain problems and solutions to the emotional and financial hurdles of providing eldercare. We'll help you define what kind of care your elderly loved one needs. We'll look at possible sources for providing that care. You'll discover that there are many types of health care available for the elderly. Many different types of living arrangements exist, including nursing homes, retirement communities, assisted living residences, and long-term care communities. We'll look at all of the options available today. We'll try to help you become a smarter consumer of eldercare services by providing you with the types of questions you'll need to ask before deciding on a course of action.

As always, money makes a difference. We will compare the cost of providing specific kinds of eldercare, from basic tasks such as bathing and driving to doctor's appointments, to choosing and paying for adult day-care centers, to hiring a "geriatric manager," to finding a suitable nursing home within your budget. We will help you identify strategies for minimizing the negative financial impact of eldercare on your budget. We will also take a look at the emotional hurdles you and your family will have to face which, if left unexamined, can undermine the effectiveness of the decisions you make and the financial plan you ultimately choose.

Finally, in the appendix of the book, we have compiled lists of national and local agencies, Federal and state programs, and associations which provide various eldercare services. We've also included toll-free numbers to save you telephone costs.

2

The Profile of a Caregiver

Let's take a closer look at Louise Gottlieb.

Louise, our hypothetical and typical baby boomer, is forty-five, married, has two children who are about to enter college, and makes about $35,000 a year, the median household income for a family of four. In reasonably good health, Louise is covered by a managed care plan through her employer, for which she pays $700 a year in premiums. The plan covers herself, her spouse, and her two children. It does not cover her mother, Alice, now sixty-five.

If Louise is lucky, she will live another forty years. And Louise's mother, Alice, will live another twenty to twenty-five years. Occasionally, when Louise and Alice have lunch at their favorite place, Friendly's on Maple Street, Louise finds herself scanning her mother's face, noting with characteristic optimism—or maybe with practiced oblivion—that her mother is still a vital and attractive woman at sixty-five. If Louise worries at all about her mother's advancing age, these butterflies are quickly shooed away by Alice's assurances that Medicare will care for her.

One day, however, something happened to Louise and Alice that happens to about two million people every year. Alice got sick. When Louise received the call from the hospital, she was so panicked that she preemptively clicked off a list of potential nightmares before the nurse could even speak—is it her heart? Her diabetes? It was a stroke. Alice had been found wandering down the aisles of the local supermarket. She was unable to recall her name, where she lived, or her phone number. It's funny how the memory works. The only thing Alice could recall in her state of confusion was that she had a daughter named Louise and that she and Louise always ate at Friendly's on Maple Street. By the way, Alice couldn't recall that Louise has two other siblings—but more on that later. The hospital tracked Louise down after the police went to the restaurant and talked to the waitresses.

Louise is now in charge of her mother's care. She loves her mother and wouldn't have it any other way. However, the daily, weekly, and monthly grind of driving her to doctor's visits and therapists, sorting out her bills, and even bathing her on those days when she is too depressed, have gradually started to wear Louise down. She has become her mother's caregiver, while still a mother to two teenagers. Pin a badge on Louise. She is now officially a member of one of the fastest growing segments of the U.S. population—the Sandwich Generation—caregivers to two generations, one ahead of them and one behind.

Obviously, something devastating and life changing has happened to Alice. She's lost the ability to speak, to travel on her own, and to live independently.

But something equally devastating and life changing has also happened to Louise. For Louise—already juggling the demanding roles of wife, mother, and wage earner—has now taken on a new role as caregiver, and this role will challenge the limits of her emotional and financial resources.

Who are these caregivers? They are the adult children—mostly women—of elderly mothers, fathers, and parents-in-law. In 1982 and 1984, the years for which the most recent data are available, the National Long-Term Care Survey commissioned by the U.S. Department of Health and Human Services reported that:

- 3.6 million Americans provided some form of primary care (e.g., bathing, cooking, shopping, paying bills) to elderly relatives living outside institutions. Of this 3.6 million, 70 percent were women, with 25 percent being wives, 25 percent daughters, and 20 percent others (e.g., daughters-in-law).
- The primary caregivers were themselves older, with an average age of fifty-seven; more than 35 percent were older than sixty-five themselves.
- Seventy-five percent of the caregivers lived with the elderly person receiving care.

- Nearly one-third of the caregivers were either poor or very close to being poor.
- About 33 percent of caregivers had health problems, rating their own health as fair or poor.

There's more. A 1987 survey commissioned by the AARP and The Travelers Foundation produced a confirming snapshot, showing that:

- More than seven million households included a caregiver (about 8 percent of all households).
- Seventy-five percent of all caregivers were women.
- Sixty-three percent of caregivers had to work for a living, either full-time or part-time, and that one-third said they had lost time from work as a result of caregiving.
- Thirty-nine percent of caregivers had children at home, meaning that these caregivers were a part of the Sandwich Generation.

Caregivers include women and men from every strata of U.S. society. And even before they were hit with the new responsibilities of providing care to elderly relatives, these caregivers were stretched. Because of the financial vise of trying to pay for college for their children, saving for retirement, paying off mortgages, they have no extra money. They have no time to spare. But they are making do.

You, too, are a caregiver if you provide unpaid help to an elderly relative. Although it's hard to determine the exact number, the Census Bureau and the AARP estimate that currently about eight million of us provide some form of help to an elderly relative every day. And that number is likely to increase dramatically for several reasons.

For one thing, America is growing older. The Census Bureau projects that as of the year 2000, the average age of all Americans will be fifty-five years old, and the life expectancy of a baby born in the year 2000 will be ninety. To put that number in perspective, consider that one hundred years ago, the average age of an American was thirty-eight years old and the life expectancy was fifty-three years old. Even as recently as the 1950s, the average age was thirty-nine years old, and the life expectancy was only sixty-eight years old. So, in roughly fifty years, our *life expectancy has almost doubled*.

You will live longer. Your parents will live longer. The time during which either you or your parents will be at an age that we used to call "old" or "elderly" is getting longer and longer. In fact, your youth and middle age will take up smaller and smaller segments of your lifespan, and, one day soon, most of your life will be lived past age fifty.

One result of the stretching of the golden years (at least we hope they will be golden) is that Americans have begun to experiment with new definitions of themselves. Like uncomfortable teenagers forced to wear their parents' old clothes, Americans are squirming as they near the ages that they used to think of as "old." They are beginning to redefine what "old" is. The fact is that more and more of us will someday face the same problems that face Louise.

These facts boil down to two startling truths. As baby boomers, we will become the largest generation of eldercare *providers* in history. And as we age, we will become the largest generation of eldercare *consumers* in history.

So, the questions that Louise faces as she deals with how to provide the best care for her mother are likely to become questions that you will need to answer yourself one day—for your parent's sake and for yourself.

PART ONE

Planning Ahead

3

Forming the Family Team

PLAN AHEAD

Long before your parent becomes sick, you can and should take steps to protect yourself from financial devastation and loss of freedom so that you can enjoy your own retirement, your own golden years, and your own dreams and the dreams of your children.

The first and most important step is the one you're taking now. Education. Gather as much information as you can about available eldercare options. Update the information as often as possible.

Then, and this is crucial, while your parents are still physically and mentally vital, have them help you design a plan of action. This strategy may be somewhat idealistic for many of us, because our parents are about as eager to face the prospects of their own mortality as we are. Nice way to ruin a Thanksgiving dinner.

If your parents cannot or will not face the fact that a locomotive is headed your way, you must seize control of the issue as early as possible.

We've laid out the data. The truth is that although most of us are not "only" children and that all of us have two biological parents either of whom can become infirm, chances are that only one of us will assume the bulk of the responsibility for providing eldercare. And chances are that someone will be a woman. And chances are that someone will be you.

But, even if you are male, whether or not you become the one who shoulders responsibility for your parents' care depends primarily on the family roles that you've been playing all your life.

11

Within families, as within corporations, some are more comfortable being leaders, whereas some are better at executing orders that the leader has issued. Others are best being cheerleaders, providing emotional encouragement, and perhaps financial support.

It may be easier to figure out which task should be assigned to each family member by taking into account:

- their abilities;
- their interest in doing a particular task;
- the state of their physical and emotional health;
- how many other responsibilities they have;
- their availability; and
- their ability to provide overtime.

It's important at this stage to be as frank and nonjudgmental about each of your strengths and weaknesses as possible. There may be many variations in personalities, styles, and strengths represented in your family, and in order for you to build the best caregiver team, it will be necessary to recognize, honor, and make use of all of these.

Some examples of common personality styles you may recognize in your family members are listed below.

Avoiders are the ones who sit silently when a problem or crisis arises. When someone asks for a volunteer, they may grow uncomfortable and look down at the dinner table. If they know in advance that a family crisis is going to be discussed, they may make an excuse not to attend. "Gosh, flu is running all through the house. I'd love to be there but I don't want to infect anybody." If you tell them you'll reschedule the meeting, they'll reschedule their flu. And if you finally manage to corner them around the dinner table, they'll eat while you talk. They'll go to the bathroom while you agonize over solutions. They'll take a smoke while you vote on whose house Mom should live in. Interestingly enough, they may love Mom as much as anyone else but they simply lack the skills or ability to confront issues head on.

Then, there's the sibling—let's call him the Supervisor—who recognizes that there's a problem but assumes that someone else will take care of it. They are great at delegating. Always have been. Take care of Mom or Dad? Who me? I'd love to but I've got that committee, I'm heading for the Chamber of Commerce, and, well, you know that would naturally interfere with any time I'd be able to give to the folks. And I wouldn't want to shortchange the folks. Besides, you've always been so much better at that sort of thing.

Another type of sibling is the one who will go along with anything that anybody else decides, so long as they don't have to take the leadership reins. Unfortunately, providing eldercare means taking leadership.

That brings us to you. Chances are that you probably are what we might call a Rescuer because you bought this book. Rescuers rush in to save the situation regardless of how bad it gets. Rescuers can't bear the thought of leaving Mom and Dad unattended to and can't bear it when a problem is left unsolved. They feel *they* can find the solution. Problems flow naturally to their doors because their doors are always open. While other siblings may be able to live with themselves if they don't help to figure out a plan for Mom or Dad, Rescuers simply cannot live with an unsolved problem or with an image of themselves as selfish or uncaring.

Once you've defined the family roles, the next step is to enlist the support of your siblings. Begin by having a family meeting.

TIPS FOR HOLDING THE FAMILY MEETING

1. Include family members who are willing to provide care—either by performing an assigned task or providing financial support—and who will be involved directly or indirectly in your relative's care. In addition, spouses or partners whose lives will be significantly affected by the plans that you're making should also attend the meeting.
2. Set clear, reachable goals for each meeting.
3. Be clear and realistic about your relative's condition before the meeting. This is not the time to get stuck on making everyone face up to the fact that Aunt Mindy has dementia. The meeting is the time to plan what to *do* about her dementia. Sooner or later, however, regardless of whether everyone has accepted that the problem exists, you'll have to have a meeting.
4. You'll probably need to meet more than once, so state this at the outset. This will help keep people from feeling tense or worried that everything has to be accomplished at once.

5. Don't try to make a decision about every issue at one meeting. Some problems will warrant further research and thought. For example, you may need to make some phone calls about a particular service before deciding who in the family has to do more.

6. Plan an agenda and stick to it. Each family member should include a short list of what they wish to discuss during the meeting. The leader of the meeting should put these in order and let everyone know all the topics that will be discussed at that particular meeting.

7. Discuss what type of help your relative needs. Be detailed. Don't just say, "Father needs help in the morning." Be specific. "He needs someone to lift him out of bed. But he can shower with a bath chair. He needs help getting out of the shower. He can dress himself, but it takes him awhile. He likes to do this on his own. Then he wants someone to help him settle in his favorite chair while he has his tea and toast."

8. Choose a "facilitator"—the person who runs the meeting. This is not necessarily the person who does all the talking. In fact, this person's role is to make sure that everything on the agenda receives attention.

9. Each person should be given a chance to talk. The others must listen without interrupting. Then, constructive responses should be given. Don't denigrate someone else's idea. Instead, think of another way to solve the problem. Look at their idea to see what parts of it might work. Make suggestions about how something could be done differently.

10. A Cardinal Rule—don't argue. Try to remain calm. Make sure you are trying to understand the other person's point of view. Try not to let old hurts, grudges, and conflicts get in the way of solving problems.

11. Focus on your relatives' needs. Keep in mind that you're trying to devise a plan to best meet his or her needs.

By the end of the meeting you should have:

1. Designated the family advocate. This person is the liaison between the agencies and individuals who are taking care of your relative and the family. When there is a problem, for example, the social worker will get a phone call from the family

advocate, not from all twenty members of your family. This also ensures that communication is clear.

2. Compiled a telephone list of family members and their phone numbers. Each person calls the person who is listed after them on the list with information received from the family member listed just above them. This way one person doesn't have to call everyone.

3. Scheduled the next meeting. Remember to make a copy of what was discussed in the meeting and give a copy to everyone who attended.

Reassess your plans periodically to make sure that things are still working well. Recognize that situations change in our lives. While your sister may have been able to come over in the morning to help your mother in the past, now that she has a new job and has to be at work thirty minutes earlier, stopping by to help Mom is really too stressful for her now. Can another arrangement be made?

If you can't get your siblings to accept shared responsibility, then at least get your parents to adjust to the coming reality that you will bear a disproportionate amount of the eldercare load. Explain to your parents that you will need more of their living or after-death estate than your siblings to compensate you for using a larger portion of your current living estate to care for them. That's only fair. Use language that is as diplomatic or as straightforward as you will need.

If you can't convince your parents or siblings to pay you for assuming this tremendous financial load—either by shifting assets from your parent's expected estate or giving cash now—*do not use your own money*. You'll only end up impoverishing yourself or robbing your children of their future.

Work out an agreement, in writing, with your siblings, acknowledging that you've had or tried to have discussions with them about your parents' eldercare, that you're willing to undertake the management of the eldercare, but that it will mean extra expense. Make up a sample projection of costs.

These are only made-up costs based on a guesstimate of how much each task would cost if you had to hire some outsider to do the things you are doing. It's a way to at least recognize the value of what you're doing on behalf of all your siblings and the entire family. The sample budget we've made up adds up to about $42,940 per year in costs. That would be $42,940 a year out of your time or pocket.

Make up your own sample projected budget using the form at the beginning of the next chapter. As we go through the book, you'll have a chance to refine your projected budget with new, better information.

Once your sample budget is created, share it with your siblings. This is the pie. Now, divide it up. Maybe a simple division of equal shares makes sense. Maybe it works better in your family if the sibling making the most money pays a slightly bigger slice of the pie. Let your family's dynamics be a factor in how you divide up the pie. But you must divide it. To do otherwise—to eat the whole cost yourself—is, for most of us, emotional and financial disaster.

4

Preparing a Budget

Caring for an elderly loved one can quickly drain your financial resources. Studies show that most of us have few resources to drain. You may be shocked to learn that, according to the 1990 U.S. Census, the last year for which data are available, the average net worth for all Americans under age sixty-five was $31,000. Considering that the cost of nursing home care in some parts of the country exceeds $100,000 per year and that providing just basic care can cost $10,000 per year, it's clear that deciding to undertake care for a relative is one of the most serious financial decisions you will ever make.

In Chapters 20–21, we will explain the options available for paying for eldercare costs.

But, before we reach the issue of payment, it will be necessary and useful to prepare a budget that itemizes the cost of providing the specific kind of care your relative needs. As we show you in this chapter, the first step is to identify each kind of care your relative requires on a daily, weekly, and monthly basis.

PROJECTION OF ELDERCARE COSTS

Assuming Mom or Dad does not require nursing care

Daily Duties	*Estimated Cost*
1. Driving to Senior Day Care Center	$_____
2. Meals	$_____
3. Bathing and other grooming	$_____
4. Interactive plan	$_____
5. Total daily expenses	$_____
6. Multiply line 5 by 3 and enter total	$_____

Monthly Duties	
7. Driving to doctor's office	$_____
8. Filling prescriptions	$_____
9. Reconciling medical billing	$_____
10. Reconciling pension payments	$_____
11. Paying for medical costs not covered by any insurance plan (e.g., Medicare)	$_____

Yearly Duties	
12. Total monthly expense	$_____
13. Multiply line 12 by 12 and enter total	$_____
14. Tax returns	$_____
15. Vacations	$_____
16. Shopping for holiday gifts	$_____
17. Total	$_____

Total Income from All Sources	
1. Social Security check	$_____
2. Pension	$_____
3. Investment income	$_____
4. Other income (such as from sale of assets or reverse mortgage—see Chapter 21)	$_____
5. Contributions or gifts from siblings and other family members	$_____

Reconciliation	
1. Total yearly income	$_____
2. Total yearly expenses (add lines 5, 13, and 17)	$_____

5

Deciding What's Needed—The Daily Skills Checklist

Before you can shop for services—or decide to handle eldercare yourself—you have to determine exactly what kind of care your elder needs. It's not as easy as you may think.

To understand what type of care your relative needs, you need to develop a precise understanding of their abilities. After all, we perform most daily activities automatically, without thinking of them as what they really are—a series of multiple, discrete tasks integrated into a complex movement. Take, for example, the action of cooking. To cook, we use our *vision* to identify raw foods and measure, we use *touch* to sense heat and turgidity, our sense of *smell* to determine when something is burning, our dexterity to hold plates and manage hot pots without scalding, wrist and arm strength, and so on. It may seem too simplistic to look at activities in this manner but it is absolutely necessary.

Detailing the basic activities your relative can perform will not only help you set up a care plan but, as you will see later on, it will also help determine whether he or she is eligible for certain kinds of Federal assistance such as Medicare programs. As precisely as you can, describe the daily activities your loved one finds difficult to perform. Activities should be thought of as *macroskills*, such as eating, which are made up of many different *microskills*. We have constructed the following checklist to help you:

Macroskills	Microskills	Level of Need		
		No Help Needed	*Some Help Needed*	*Total Help Needed*
Eating	Hold utensils			
	Spoon, fork, or carve food			
	Swallow, chew			
Bathing	Balance to get into tub			
	Balance and strength to get out of tub			
	Strength to turn on/off faucet			
	Flexibility to bathe			
Paying bills and managing money	Memory			
	Ability to calculate to avoid over-spending			
	Basic organizational skills			
Taking medication	Memory			
	Dexterity			
Shopping	Ability to walk or be mobile with walker, wheelchair, or other device			
	Manage money and make change			
	Make decisions			

Macroskills	Microskills	Level of Need		
		No Help Needed	*Some Help Needed*	*Total Help Needed*
Telephone	Memory			
	Hearing			
	Ability to speak			
	Ability to dial or cradle phone			
Cooking and food preparation	Memory			
	Vision			
	Awareness of temperature			
	Awareness of dietary needs			
	Smell to sense burning or spoilage			
Housekeeping	Physical strength and stamina			
	Agility			
	Vision			
	Memory			
	Awareness to avoid safety hazards, e.g., mixing chemicals such as chlorine and detergent			

This level of detail may seem painfully tedious but it will help you accomplish two goals. First, you'll avoid overbuying. Breaking down services into components will help you to better identify what you *don't* need as well as what you do need.

Second, the exercise of identifying exactly what your loved one can accomplish will help you understand his or her frustration in losing parts of the bundle of capabilities that define who they are. Perhaps, more importantly, the process will also help you see what your loved one can still do and to applaud those capabilities.

It should be noted that you do not have to decide which kind of care is needed on your own. If you'd prefer and if you can afford it, you could have an outsider help you make these decisions. "Geriatric care managers" sometimes called "geriatric case managers" will, for a fee, evaluate your elderly loved one's ability to perform activities of daily living, monitor the care provided, and act either as the primary or supplemental family advocate. Such care managers can be especially helpful in those situations where the elderly loved one lives in another town or community, making it difficult for you to interact with and plan for them on your own.

Where do you find a good geriatric care manager? A good place to start is the National Association of Professional Geriatric Care Managers, 1609 N. Country Club Rd., Tucson, Arizona 85716. Their phone number is (602) 881-8008.

6

What Are the Options?

Elderly people who choose not to live with or be cared for by a family member have several available options. Depending on the level of assistance needed, this care can range from fairly minimal assistance provided by hiring outside care to supplemental in-home care, to intermediate care facilities or residential care facilities, to the extreme end of the range of dependent care provided in skilled nursing facilities. Listed below are the current options available at present. Each of these will be discussed in greater detail in a separate chapter devoted to each option:

- Assisted living residences
- Intermediate care residences
- Nursing homes
- Long-term care communities
- Use of community services
- Hospice care

Here's an overview of each option.

ASSISTED LIVING RESIDENCES

If your relative is in good physical health, but needs help with macroskills such as bathing, dressing, eating, or remembering to take medication, an assisted living residence might be the perfect solution.

23

INTERMEDIATE CARE FACILITIES

Residents in an intermediate care facility have chronic health conditions that do not require intensive nursing care. The staff in these facilities generally consists of licensed practical nurses and nurse's aides.

RESIDENTIAL CARE FACILITIES

Residential care facilities are for those who have not experienced a major decline in mental or physical condition, but who need assistance with tasks such as eating, bathing, and dressing. Medicare and Medicaid eligibility requirements for acceptance into these facilities vary according to state.

NURSING HOMES

Placement in a skilled nursing facility is indicated when there is a need for extensive nursing or rehabilitative care. In this type of facility, a registered nurse works with a physician on a regular basis to monitor and provide care.

COMMUNITY SERVICES

Many communities offer a range of services to homebound or elderly residents at no cost or for a low fee. These services are valuable to the elderly and their families. You get some peace of mind in knowing that your loved one is being cared for, and your loved one will benefit from the greater sense of independence because they won't have to rely on you for everything.

PART TWO

You as the Caregiver

7

Emotional and Practical Considerations

PLANNING AHEAD—PRACTICAL CONSIDERATIONS

Many factors will affect your decision regarding whether to assume the role of caregiver.

For one thing, you may not live near your elderly loved one. Or, you may not have the financial resources to take on the job, even after factoring in contributions from other siblings. Your resources may be depleted because of divorce, college costs, or your own health problems and those of your spouse.

Likewise, you probably have a job outside your home. So, you will not be able to provide certain kinds of care that your elderly loved one may need such as driving to doctor's offices or adult day-care centers.

But, even if you are willing and able to provide home care to your loved one, the simple truth is that he or she may not welcome your help. Like all of us, older people cherish their independence. Independence is vital to preserving self-respect, and dignity, and is even linked to longevity and mental alertness. Independence is to be encouraged, provided that it doesn't endanger your loved one's health.

If your elderly loved one can handle living alone, let it happen. Support it. But deciding whether your loved one can handle living alone is itself tricky. How do you judge? In fact, who *should be judging*? Here are some objective criteria to help you, your loved one, or both of you make that decision.

First, try to look at your loved one in terms of the skills they have. As discussed in Chapter 5, certain basic skills are necessary for independent living:

- Can she navigate familiar territory (e.g., home, neighborhood community) without getting lost?
- Can she cook for herself without high risk of burning or cutting?
- Can he bathe himself and get in and out of bathtubs or showers unassisted?
- Can she groom her hair?
- Can she brush her teeth?
- Can he shop for food alone?
- Can she still make change correctly and, in general, is she organized about her finances, remembering to pay bills?
- Can he go to the toilet without soiling himself? Is he incontinent?
- Can she remember to take her medication in the correct dosage and on time?
- Can he tell a joke or story appropriately, without flubbing the punchline or repeating it endlessly?
- Will she get lost if unaccompanied on shopping trips?
- Does she wander out of the house and forget how to get back home?
- Can he clean the house and take care of business matters independently?
- If suffering from an illness, is he able to provide the prescribed care routine for himself?
- Is she in any way a physical danger to herself or others?
- Will she be safe if left unsupervised, or is around-the-clock care needed?
- Has she shown signs of forgetfulness, confusion, or dementia?

Consult your relative's physician to discuss any changes in symptoms, mood, behavior, or health that you notice. It's especially important to list any inability to perform any of the functions listed above. Family members should meet to discuss the problem and to make a joint decision about what steps to take. If it's not possible to meet in person, then arrange a telephone conference or send a letter so that each family member who has input is indeed given an opportunity to express it.

PLANNING AHEAD—EMOTIONAL CONSIDERATIONS

The decision to become a caregiver is one of the most important decisions in your life.

It's as life changing as the decision to marry or the decision to have a child.

Moreover, it will have a long range effect on the lives of everyone in your household. So, for the sake of everyone involved, do not make this decision quickly. And certainly do not make the decision without carefully weighing all issues and options.

Caregiving is a little like running a marathon, except that this marathon has to be run every day. And you feel like it's your duty to smile while you're running. And it's possible that the effort will never get recognized or appreciated by anyone but you.

Because it's a marathon, because you don't really have time to run it, and because no matter how fast or well you run it, no one's there to applaud, caregiving can be extremely stressful. How stressful?

We all have just so much in our emotional well. Stress draws buckets from that well. We can take just so much stress.

The stress you feel as a caregiver is likely to increase as the need for care increases. Your life and the lives of those who are connected to your life will become more complicated.

And, perhaps most importantly, your time and freedom will be significantly restricted.

For all these reasons, there will be times when you may feel angry, resentful, burned out, exhausted, and overwhelmed—all symptoms of what some people call "compassion fatigue." These feelings are usual and can be alleviated with the help of a good support system. Part Three will detail the kinds of support you can find in your area.

8

Moving Mom In

PROVIDING CARE IN YOUR HOME

You've had the family meeting and you've agreed to be the primary caregiver for your parent. We'll refer to the recipient of care as "Mom" in our examples below. However, many of the same issues apply if you're providing care for another adult family member or friend.

Many practical problems must be resolved before your relative can move into your home. You will probably have to sort through many emotional issues as well.

In this chapter, we will examine some of the practical hurdles that you may have to face. Then, we will help you sort through the emotional ups and downs of caregiving.

Practical Considerations of Caregiving
- Is there adequate space in your home for an added person?
- If not, can more space be built or made by changing the way that the rooms are used?
- Is your schedule already too full or emotionally demanding to take on another responsibility?
- Are you the parent of young children?
- Are you a single parent?
- Are you already responsible for a physically disabled person?
- Is your present job demanding, time-consuming, or stressful?
- Are you suffering from a physical or emotional illness?
- What community resources are available?

- Is your relative eligible for publicly funded sources of support?
- Does your relative have a medical condition that will require you to provide care?

Do You Have Space Available for Your Parent?

Preferably, Mom should have her own bedroom. Ideally, her room would be large enough to have a sitting area, where she can read, do a hobby, or watch television. Is there a window in her room?

Also, you'll need to safety-proof your home. Changes in Mom's vision and agility can cause tripping and accidents.

Think about safety precautions that may be needed in every room. We've listed some in the Table below. It's not an all-inclusive list but it will get you started along the path of thinking and planning for safety.

SAFETY CONSIDERATIONS	
Bathroom	– non-slip mats on floor and in tub.
	– guard rails in tub/shower.
	– well-lit so that she can see.
	– ability to rise from that height.
Bedroom	– telephone with large numbers and a list of emergency numbers.
	– non-slip mats (throw away scatter rugs).
	– well-lit.
	– comfortable chair.
	– television with remote and volume control.
	– comfortable mattress.
	– good ventilation.
	– warm enough in autumn/winter.
	– cool enough in spring/summer.
Kitchen	– use stove safety conditions.
	– hazardous cleaners must be stored safely.

Can You Assume More Responsibility?

If your daily schedule is demanding or time-consuming (and whose schedule is not these days?), you simply may not have the time to take care of your relative. You be the judge. If your cup of daily hassles is almost full but not to the brim, consider using adult day-care services, home health care workers, or senior citizen centers to help out. But if your cup of daily hassle has already runneth over—you're rarely home or cannot assume the obligation to come home to provide the care your relative needs—other options are better choices for you.

Are You Faced with the Demands of Parenthood?

Combining the roles of caregiver to your mom and parent to your children is, as we've said, a gargantuan task both emotionally and practically. There are some pluses and, of course, plenty of minuses. If you are the parent of young children or if you are a single parent, you can still be a caregiver. However, you'll benefit from using the support services that are available.

On the plus side, having an elderly loved one in the home can enhance the interconnectedness of your children to their grandmother. Your children will have an opportunity to relate more closely to your mom. They'll also have many more opportunities to talk, share histories, learn from and do things with one another—all of which will enrich and deepen family bonds. From your mom's perspective, children and teenagers can bring a gaiety to her life that she might have missed. Because grandchildren are reflections and extensions of her, they may ease some of the stress she may be feeling with the growing advances of her own mortality and frailty. Grandchildren can help her feel *needed*.

The disadvantages are that your children may resent your mom's presence. They may act out in frustration and anger because of the need to make sacrifices such as giving up their bedroom or having to share your attention.

Are You Physically Disabled?

If you are suffering from a physical illness or a chronic health condition, you may not be physically able to provide care. But if you want your loved one to live with you despite your limitations, hire outside help, such as a home care worker. Or you can help your relative arrange to go to an adult day-care center a few times per week. Living together can be beneficial to both of you. So, if that's what you wish, don't automatically assume it can't be done. Consider hiring a geriatric care manager to coordinate the best plan for your relative.

Have Other Family Members Agreed to Help You?

Even if you've been designated as "primary caregiver," others on the caregiving team should be viewed as "secondary or ancillary caregivers." Everybody's got a job in this business of caregiving. You've got yours. And they've got theirs. Don't let people off the hook. Remember, even though Mom is coming to live with you, if it has been decided that your relatives will help you care for her, they must be expected to meet their end of the agreement. You'll recall our advice to write out the care plan, including who's responsible for what and when they are supposed to do it. Stick to this plan. We've included a sample (Fig. A). If confusion or disagreement arises later—and it almost inevitably will—you can refer to the written plan.

Sometimes, when problems arise, families seek help from a social worker or a professional counselor to mediate and provide an objective intervention. Or, you can have another family meeting. These meetings are a useful way to open up and talk about each other's feelings, problems, and accomplishments. Make sure you talk about what's been working out right as well as what's been going wrong. Family members can thus see for themselves that your caregiving team can accomplish its goals.

You can include your mom in the family meetings *if* it's not a gripe session about how difficult she is making your life. Be sensitive to her presence if she's home during the meeting and don't complain aloud. Focus on finding solutions rather than simply stating the problem.

Name	Task	When
Mary	Drive Mother to the physical therapist and then take her back home	Every Wednesday and Thursday 6–7 P.M.
Tom	Call pharmacy about prescription, pick up medication on the way home from work, and then take them to Mother	Every Friday 8 A.M. (call 6:30 P.M. to talk to mother)
James	Drive Mother to the beauty salon	Every Saturday 10 A.M.
Mary	Take Mother home from beauty salon	Saturday 11:30 A.M.

FIGURE A Family Plan for Caring for Mother

If your parent has a medical condition that requires the use of medical instruments or equipment, ask yourself, "Will I truly be comfortable handling the instruments I'll need to provide Mom with the care she needs?" Do needles or blood make you squeamish? Can you really learn to use and read monitors and gauges, give medication, or administer needles as prescribed? Then there's the big issue of touching Mom's body.

Providing physical care often involves touching and seeing parts of your mom's body that she has kept private all her life. This experience is often awkward and difficult for all, and requires adjustment. It is helpful to acknowledge the awkwardness you feel in such a situation and encourage your mom to do the same. Then, address the necessity for providing the care and encourage your relative to assist you whenever possible so that her feelings of self-dignity and independence are supported.

Rather than deal with these squeamish issues yourself, you may decide to hire a home health care attendant to help bathe your mother. A nurse may come by to check her blood pressure or medication. We discuss these services in Chapter 13. They can be important supplements to your caregiving.

The quality of your relationship with your relative prior to this stage in life can be an indicator of how you can negotiate the issues that come up now that you're living together. The conflicts that existed previously in your relationship, but weren't resolved, may crop up again now.

The Emotional Considerations of Caregiving

Even once the practical aspects of caregiving are worked out, you and Mom might wonder whether this kind of arrangement can really work. Your feelings about being a caregiver—and your mom's feelings about needing care—will influence the outcome. Here are some questions you should ask yourself:

- Have you been able to live with your loved one in the past or get along with him or her in general?
- Do you consider your marriage or partnership stable enough to withstand the stress caused by being a caregiver?
- Are you emotionally stable? Or have you been prone to suffer from debilitating depression, anxiety, or other emotional problems?

For example, although Ann may have always disliked her mother's tendency to be "bossy," she was able to ignore it once she left for college and they no longer lived together. Now that they are considering living together once again, this conflict may resurface and, depending on whether they have made changes in their personalities, it could cripple any chances they have of working out a living arrangement.

In addition, Ann's husband and children will have feelings about watching her interact with her mother. Their feelings about this are likely to affect their relationships with Ann. For example, Ann's husband may not like it when she acquiesces to her mother's request for nonessential care because, in his view, it keeps her from being able to meet his needs. Alternatively, he may worry that Ann is overextending herself and causing herself harm. Her children may not fully understand why Ann so often is tired, worried, or distracted.

Although it's not always possible to fully resolve conflicts among family members, it may be possible to decide how to relate comfortably to one another in order to live together once again.

In a parent–child relationship, when the parent has had problems such as alcohol abuse or was physically or emotionally abusive to the "child," it's often not possible to resolve the feelings about these experiences sufficiently to enable the parent and "child" to live together again.

If you have this type of history with your parent, you certainly have the option of walking away from it all. There's nothing written on your birth certificate that requires you to navigate through memories that are just too painful to you all for the sake of helping your once-abusive parent. However if, despite your history, you still wish to help your parent, then change your goals. Instead of having your parent live with you, focus on providing certain types of services. Steer away from emotional interchanges that can stir up feelings of conflict.

As you might expect, the relationship you develop with your parent when he or she comes to live with you will be very different from the relationship you've had previously. The same issues might exist but now that you're an adult you can choose to deal with them differently. Both you and your relative will have to make significant adjustments to enable you to live together harmoniously.

We tend to think that taking care of an adult relative is the same as taking care of a child. However, caring for an elderly person is considerably different—and in some ways even more difficult—than caring for a child. Because your relative is now an adult, she has already developed various personality attributes, values, opinions, and habits. She may not want to change the aspects of herself that you don't like. As the caregiver, you may find it hard to live with your mother's bossiness or her opinionated manner of speaking.

Even though your relationship is now a parent–adult child relationship, your parent may not want to relinquish the all-important "upper hand." Your parent may still have the view that her way is the right way and that you as the "child" should acquiesce. But, of course, you are no longer a child. You've established a household of your own. You may have raised children. You earn a paycheck. You pay taxes and bills. You have rightfully grown accustomed to being in charge. You're certainly not going to retreat to a status as "child" again, regardless of how noble the motives.

It's a challenge to maintain your position as head of household while also supporting your parent's effort to feel self-sufficient and in control of her life. However, there is a difference between letting your parent maintain independence and control of her own life and letting her take control of your life.

You now have two households merged into one. Similar to having two chefs in one kitchen, you'll both feel that someone's got to go—or change.

Change—and willingness to adapt to the situation—will make it easier for everyone to get along. Each person needs to try to understand the other person's views and preferences. You are also going to feel a sense of loss. Your parent may no longer seem to be quite the same to you.

For example, you may have become accustomed to calling your father for financial advice or talking with your mother about the difficulty of combining the demands of career with parenthood. Now, your mother may be more focused on her health problems. As a result, she may be less emotionally available to you. You're likely to miss this part of your relationship. You'll experience the change as a significant loss.

But, from Mom's perspective, she's also experiencing major losses. And asserting her need for the upper hand may be her way of compensating for other losses. In her world, she may no longer perceive any gains, only losses.

The aging process is characterized by changes in our physical and emotional state. And most of these changes are experienced as losses. We lose our jobs due to retirement. We lose parents; we lose spouses. Your best friend Harry, who always used to laugh at your jokes, is gone. Died two years ago. Now, who'll laugh at your jokes the way Harry used to. We lose our "best physical selves," the self who could run and climb all day, remember everything and everybody; the one who could hear and see clearly and who could exist without piles of pills. The one who could dance without pain. Our "best selves" are replaced by a body that always complains. What is it this week, an old heart? Chronic illnesses such as heart disease, hypertension, and arthritis wear you down little by little.

Because we become less mobile as we age, we may become increasingly isolated from friends and places. We just can't get around anymore like we used to. As isolation increases, many of us suffer from depression. The increased risk of depression is one reason why it is important that elders remain connected to social events and people throughout their lives. Without these connections, the spirit withers. Elderly people often become convinced that they no longer matter to anyone or anything. As a result, their health may decline rapidly, increasing the need for eldercare.

Tips to make life easier for everyone when your parent comes to live in your home.

- You and your spouse are heads of household. Be firm about having your parent respect this.
- Resist the urge to slip into the role of a child when relating to your parent.
- Your parent is not a visitor anymore so include him or her in the household tasks.
- Make your expectations clear—don't assume anyone will automatically know what you want.
- Maintain boundaries and respect each person's personal space. Each person is entitled to their own room; rooms such as the family room can be used communally.

- Think of solutions when problems arise. Problem solve instead of complaining or arguing.
- Talk or write—communicate when there is a problem.

Tips to help make your parent comfortable in your home.

- If possible, situate your parent so that their bedroom is near a bathroom. Otherwise you may need to purchase a portable toilet.
- Have enough table space in her bedroom so that anything she'll need is within reach (e.g., eyeglasses, water pitcher, cups, books).
- If she likes to watch television, place it in easy view, with the remote control next to her.
- If you need a hospital bed, side rails, walkers, or wheelchair, buy or rent them.
- If possible, arrange it so that your relative can have a few visitors in her room, and they can sit comfortably.

Warning Signs—you've tried it for a few months, but it's still not working.

- You feel angry, yell a lot, or have become physically abusive to your relative or other family members. Reassess whether this arrangement is best for your relative, yourself and your family.

As you put effort into caring for your parent you'll experience the loss of your time and freedom. It's likely that your parent is also feeling a sense of loss. It was probably very difficult for her to move out of her home or apartment and leave familiar surroundings. For some people, it's as though the door to one part of their life has been shut. It's a signal that their life can no longer be the same.

Help Mom develop and maintain a meaningful lifestyle to the extent that is possible. We all need a purpose to our lives. We all need to feel useful. Mom may feel socially isolated after coming to live in your home. Her friends may be unable to drive to visit. Other friends may have moved or died. Encourage Mom's friends to visit her even if it means getting someone to drive them over to your home.

Talk to Mom to learn how she's feeling. Don't make assumptions about her feelings. She may feel relief at not having to manage on her own. On the other hand, she may feel angry, sad, or resentful about all the changes she's had to make to become a part of your household. These are normal feelings and talking about them often helps to understand them.

She may feel angry and betrayed by her body because of its declining state. She may worry about illness and the dependency on others that it causes. She may find it difficult to accept that she will have to depend on someone for help for the rest of her life. Her feelings may be expressed by negative or angry behavior toward you and your family members. Out of frustration, she may simply withdraw, refusing to do even the things she is able to do. Or, she may start to complain of problems or aches and pains that she's not really feeling.

If talking with Mom does not help, seek advice from others who have had the same type of experience. Look for a support group. We've included a list of national organizations in the Appendix that can help you find a support group. You may also find that a consultation with a professional trained in gerontology or geriatric care can also be helpful. Here are some suggestions to help Mom break through her frustration:

- Share meals together. Make her a part of as many family events as you can think of.
- Recognize that sexuality is a part of all stages of life. Give her privacy when she needs it.
- Respect and encourage her desire to relate to others.
- Consult with the appropriate medical care providers, such as the audiologist or ophthalmologist, when necessary to improve her ability to function.

Depression is a common problem for the elderly. Loss and change, accompanied by aging, often leads to depression. The signs and symptoms of depression include:

- lack of energy and disinterest in activities she used to enjoy;
- talk of death or suicide;
- lack of attention given to personal hygiene and grooming;

- problems with sleeping;
- loss of appetite;
- increased use of alcohol, drugs, or tobacco; and
- persistent feelings of sadness, with no apparent cause.

Take depression seriously. Use the signs above as a guideline if you suspect depression, and remember that any major change in behavior or mood could signal the onset of depression. Encourage Mom to speak with a physician, psychotherapist, or trusted friend or relative. Depression is a treatable illness that, if left unchecked, can lead to suicidal thoughts and actions. Your physician may prescribe medication to alleviate depression. Counseling or psychotherapy are important secondary forms of treatment.

Some of the problems faced by your elderly parent may not at first be recognizable to you. In fact, your elderly parent may even not be aware of some of the changes that have occurred. For example, problems with balance, vision, or agility may make your relative more prone to falls. With advancing age, their bones become more susceptible to break than in their youth. Remind Mom not to move too suddenly when changing her position and to avoid any activities that require climbing or the use of balance.

Vision problems may have contributed to a lack of interest in Mom's usual activities. These problems also can lead to social withdrawal and social isolation. Hearing loss can cause confusion, disorientation, or paranoid behavior, making Mom believe that others are talking about her "behind my back."

The elderly often have difficulty tolerating changes in room temperature. Ask Mom if she is too warm or cold. If it's hard to find a temperature that's comfortable for everyone in the house, keep sweaters and blankets handy.

It's important that Mom be examined by a board-certified geriatrician or a physician with expertise in the care of the elderly. Usually, a nurse and social worker are also members of the geriatric care team. A thorough examination will assess Mom's physical health, mental state, and her level of functioning. You can help the process by making certain that the physician is aware of information such as:

- Mom's health history (e.g., past illnesses, injuries, hospitalizations, conditions);

- past and current use of over-the-counter and prescription medications;
- allergies and drug sensitivities;
- problems with walking (tendency to trip or fall);
- problems with vision or memory loss;
- aids used in functioning (e.g., eyeglasses, dentures, canes);
- symptoms such as dizziness, nausea, fatigue, and swelling;
- past and current emotional state—does Mom seem depressed, agitated, or anxious? Does she talk about dying despite being healthy? Does she or any of her family members have a history of depression or other psychological problems?
- impairment in her level of functioning such as persistent difficulty in sleeping, loss of appetite, unusual changes in appetite, weight gain or loss, incontinence;
- use of drugs or alcohol; and
- social isolation.

Accompany Mom to the doctor, but don't try to do all the talking for her. Remember always that she is an adult and, unless she has memory or speech problems, she will want to function independently. If you have concerns, discuss them with the physician *after* Mom has finished talking. Part of the examination is to assess your relative's speech and thought patterns, so let the physician hear from your relative.

Help Mom maintain a meaningful lifestyle to whatever extent possible. Find ways to help her maintain a sense of purpose and a feeling of usefulness.

THE DECISION: SHOULD YOUR LOVED ONE REMAIN AT HOME?

First, if Mom can help you make this decision, then by all means, let her help. By doing so, you demonstrate your respect for her opinion and her right to have a voice in matters pertaining to her life. You also acknowledge her individuality and demonstrate your awareness of her need for autonomy.

Prepare yourself for the possibility that Mom will have a hard time dealing with, or even contemplating dealing with, a change in lifestyle. Not every elderly person will feel relief or pleasure at the thought of living with and being cared for by others. Remember this. No one likes to be a burden and no one likes to be thought of as a burden.

Your elderly loved one may fear moving elsewhere. She may be fearful about losing her "things." Over time, all of us become attached to things. Things revive memories. That chair belonged to my grandmother when she was a child. I nursed my first child on that back porch in the summer time. My husband slow danced with me on that hardwood floor every Christmas night after we finished wrapping the kids' gifts. Things have life. Things give life.

Naturally, your elderly loved one will feel loss at the prospect of leaving her loved things and her loved places.

To paraphrase the poet Elizabeth Bishop, no one masters the art of losing. Not your relative. Not you. It all feels like disaster.

Recognize Mom's feelings of loss. Acknowledge these feelings by talking with her about them. Help her talk about her memories, about the lives in the things she is leaving. Maybe, after this talk, you will both realize there's too much life in those things for her to leave and still keep on being herself. Maybe you'll find a way to bring along enough of those things to celebrate her life and memories in a new setting—your joint home.

Openly acknowledging the feelings involved in this lifestyle change can make it easier to move on.

Nothing is simple about the adjustments that you and your family will have to make to accommodate an elderly loved one in your home. Even minor adjustments can become major adjustments. For example, day one starts. You've made sure all of Mom's beloved things have been placed carefully into her new room. Exhaling, you experience a wonderful moment of contentment and self-satisfaction. Pride, in fact. You've done it. You feel good about what you've done.

Soon, however, you notice that Mother is not coming out of her room very much. She seems cranky and sad. What now? It's time to talk to her about her adjustment to your home. What seems easy to you may in fact be very painful for her. She may be hesitant to join in the conversation with you and the rest of the family. That thing about knowing her place. Not overstepping bounds. Not wearing out her welcome. Or she may be confused about the layout of your home. She may just miss her old surroundings. In a nutshell, she needs your help in making the adjustment to living with you.

Personal habits are often hard to change. For example, your mother may be unable to hear the television at your usual volume setting. She may not like to hear music in the morning, a habit of your teenager that you have learned to tolerate. You'll need to decide which habits can be changed—must be changed—and which can be tolerated through compromise. As with most problems, talking and listening are the start to answering the problem. Commitment is the rest of the answer.

9

Caring for the Caregiver

We only have a certain amount of emotional and physical stamina. Caregiving will take a toll on you emotionally and physically. Providing care in your home to a loved one will place a heavy strain on your emotional and physical resources. Caregiving can be an extremely long-term open-ended commitment. You can love your parent dearly, yet find it hard to actually take care of them. The stress of caregiving is likely to increase over time, and your parent's need for care is likely to increase. Your life, and the lives of all those who are connected to yours, will be affected. You will have less time and freedom in your day to do what you want to do. That's why it's important to:

- ask for help from others;
- take care of your own physical needs;
- take time to fulfill your spiritual needs;
- take regular breaks from providing care;
- develop a network of supportive friends, family members, and community resources;
- nurture yourself;
- continue to develop your interests and hobbies;
- maintain friendships;
- take time to be alone and to focus on yourself;
- accept that you will feel angry or resentful at times;
- set limits on others; be willing to say "no"; and
- acknowledge the good that you are doing; forgive yourself for mistakes.

Ask for help from others. We've described the necessity of enlisting family members to take responsibility for doing specific tasks. Don't hesitate to ask for more help from others. Ask friends and neighbors to help you in specific ways. For example, if your mother needs support hose for her aching legs and you know that your neighbor usually drives past the store which sells them, ask your neighbor if she would mind stopping in and purchasing some for you. Don't feel guilty about needing help. You've assumed a huge responsibility, and you'll be better equipped to help your parent if you don't feel overwhelmed from having to do everything yourself.

It may not occur to you that there are many small tasks that someone else could do for you to help make your life and your parent's life far more pleasant. Like many people, you probably have become accustomed to being self-sufficient. This is not the time, or the way, to show your independence.

In good neighborly fashion, reciprocate when you can. If you or your mother like to bake, make a cake or pie for the neighbor who thoughtfully came by with your parent's favorite magazine or went to the store at your request. You don't need to reciprocate with family members, and don't feel guilty when they help you. Remember, you're in the same family, working toward a common goal of helping a relative.

Take care of your own physical needs. If you become tired and overly stressed, you won't be able to take care of your parent. The quality of life for her and for yourself will suffer. Your spouse and children will feel the effect of this as well, because you'll become emotionally or physically unavailable to them.

Establish and maintain a regular exercise schedule. This will help you feel better physically and mentally. While you're focusing on your exercise, you can't focus on the chores or problems you're having with your mother. Exercise will also improve your strength and endurance and help you to withstand the rigors of caregiving. Take time to have a soothing bath. Don't simply rush from work to doing chores and then jump into bed, expecting to be able to rest in a way that replenishes your body.

Resist the temptation to eat on the run. Eat a balanced diet. Caregivers tend to forget about the importance of eating the proper foods. Take the time to have a manicure or a facial.

Take time to fulfill your spiritual needs. If you were accustomed to attending religious services, ask someone to stay with your relative while you do this. If prayer or meditation was part of your daily routine, don't stop just so that you can "save" that time and do a chore instead. Our spiritual beliefs are a source of strength. If you have incorporated religion or spirituality into your life, don't let it go now. If it has helped you before, it can certainly help you now. You will need this source of strength, faith, and hope in the days and months ahead.

As emphasized throughout this book, caregivers need care too. This means that you have to establish a support network so that when you need a break, someone is available to fill that position temporarily.

Using respite care is a must for caregivers. It gives you time away from your caregiving responsibilities. Take this time to recharge your batteries—you'll need it in the days and weeks to come.

Respite care can be provided in a number of different forms. You could pay someone to watch your relative while you go out for a few hours or take a trip. You could use your friends or family members to also help you have some free time. Many nursing homes, hospitals, and assisted living residences provide temporary lodging for respite care for a few days or a few weeks. You could seek the services of hospice care workers or home health care workers. The cost of respite care varies tremendously, depending primarily on the nature of the person's condition and their insurance eligibility. Many caregivers use respite on a routine basis, building it into their care plan. This is a good idea, especially if you're often busy or if you know you'll want or need to be away from home periodically.

Take regular respites from providing care. Family members, friends, and home health care workers can watch your elderly parent and provide care while you take a short break or even go away on vacation. Everyone needs a rest from their responsibilities from time to time.

Develop a support network. Think of yourself as the manager of a small company, whose goal is to provide care for your relative. Figure out what each person in the "company" can do to reach this goal, based on their abilities, interests, and strengths. In general, people are more willing to do something when they feel confident that they can do it well. If you know that Mr. Adams likes to drive, ask him to help out in this way. Since Tara, the teenager down the street, likes to do volunteer work, and she enjoys reading, ask if she'd be willing to read to your mother for a half hour each week.

Don't forget to use the community resources such as transportation services and senior citizen centers. In many communities, tuition-free programs are available to elderly residents. If your parent is not cognitively disabled, he or she might enjoy attending a class in a college setting. Then, instead of depending totally on you to be her link to the outside world of information, she will come home with news to tell you. Best of all, she will feel vital and interesting.

Caregivers also benefit when their relatives are able to use senior centers and adult day-care centers. For many families, this lets the caregiver continue working while knowing that their parent is in a safe, stimulating environment.

Nurture yourself. Even if others don't always do as you asked them to do to help you, there are ways you can help yourself. Seek pleasure in your daily life. Buy yourself flowers. Listen to your favorite music. Send daily affirmations to yourself. Say to yourself "I am worthwhile" or "I am doing the best I can."

Continue to develop your interests and hobbies. Time is always a problem for the caregiver who has many responsibilities and obligations. Don't put your interests on hold while caring for a relative. You may no longer be able to attend computer class four nights per week as you have in the past, but you can find a course that meets once per week for a few hours. Then, if you can, schedule a family member or friend to handle the task of caring for your relative during this time.

You might feel uncomfortable about letting family or friends know that you need their help so that you can enjoy a nonessential activity or hobby. Remind yourself that you are entitled to live your own life. Surround yourself with people who support this goal.

Maintain friendships. It's easy to let friendships fall to the side when we're busy with family. However, friendships are an important part of our lives. Keep in contact with your friends. Phone them regularly and take time to talk with them. It's okay to request that they call only during a specific time each day. For example, one woman's telephone answering machine stated: "We're busy at the moment so please leave your name and number. Or call us again between the hours of six thirty and eight o'clock in the evening. We'll be able to talk to you then." By doing this, she let callers know that she wanted to talk to them and specified when she'd be able to do so. This is better than hurriedly calling a friend and being brusque because you feel pressured to get off the phone and fix dinner. In time, your friends and neighbors will get accustomed to your schedule. They may even develop a schedule of their own once they recognize the usefulness and time-saving aspects.

A word of caution. Caregivers are often tempted to rely on their spouse to give them a break from caring for a relative. While a spouse should have a role in providing care, don't overuse your spouse. You'll both burn out fast. Instead, take time out from caregiving to spend together. Maintain your marriage or partnership. Take time to replenish it. Take time to talk with one another about topics other than the care that you're providing.

Accept that at times you feel angry or resentful about your caregiving responsibilities. Talk to people who understand what you're going through. Join a support group. You'll be surprised to hear how others feel. You'll learn that negative feelings are normal, even if they make you feel that you're not "nice." You'll see that other "nice" people have these feelings too. Those who are also caregivers can truly understand what you're going through.

Set limits: Say "no." Set limits in all parts of your life. Determine for yourself what is reasonable to expect from yourself. Don't allow others to take advantage of you or talk you into doing something you don't want—or don't have time—to do.

Also set limits on your parent. Don't feel that you have to do everything for her or be everything to her. Encourage her to do as much as possible for herself.

If you don't take care of yourself, you'll become like a robot moving from task to task without taking time to enjoy the pleasures in your life. You may have stopped nurturing yourself or others in your family who also deserve nurturance or attention from you. The problem is that you can only do so many things in one day. Set priorities and be flexible. What works today may not work tomorrow. When something needs to be done, examine your options with a flexible frame of mind. For example, if you need to take your son to piano lessons at the same time your parent has a doctor's appointment, find out if you can carpool with another parent. Or, see if the senior citizens' transportation service in your town can come and get your mother.

Sometimes, despite the best of plans, stress builds up, and you feel overloaded. Yet, you continue on, feeling that you "should" be able to handle it all. Your body will probably send signals to you letting you know that it needs a time out.

The following list contains the warning signs that should tell you that you need to reduce the stress of caregiving and take a break:

- You have persistent difficulty eating or sleeping.
- You feel anxious, cranky, irritable, or overwhelmed at the start of each day.
- You notice (or someone tells you) that you've begun to abuse alcohol or to smoke excessively.
- You lose or gain a lot of weight.
- You lose interest in your appearance or find that you no longer take the time to groom yourself.
- You find yourself acting harshly or abusively to your relative or others in your life.
- You have recurrent thoughts of death or suicide.

Don't give up. There are steps you can take to start feeling better.

- Use respite care and take a vacation or a short break.
- Stop turning down help that is offered.
- Begin a physician-approved exercise program.
- Join a support group. Don't feel embarrassed to relate your experiences. Chances are that others there have probably had similar experiences. Members of a support group can also provide you with valuable information and resources to help you and your loved one.
- Seek professional help from a counselor, psychotherapist, or psychiatrist.

10

Caregiving: Special Challenges

DEMENTIA

Taking care of a parent or relative who suffers from dementia is a difficult, frustrating, often anger-provoking task. Your relative may seem like a stranger to you. He or she may have a new or different personality—one that you have never seen before. You may not like the person she seems to have become. You may wonder where the person you knew and loved has gone.

People with dementia often behave in strange or confusing ways. One minute they're calm and content, while the next minute they are screaming angrily. Your relative may have been neat and meticulous all of his life. Now, he is unshaven and unbathed.

It's crucial that you take time to take care of yourself. This will help you keep sane when everything seems to be going wrong.

Unfortunately, however, with dementia things don't usually get better as time goes on. So you need to prepare yourself, your family, and your relative for a difficult, harsh future. Because suffering from dementia places your relative at a high risk of unknowingly harming themselves, safety precautions are crucial.

Installing safety measures in your home is the easy part. It is coping emotionally with living with a relative who suffers from dementia that's the hard part.

Safety tips for living with persons with dementia:

- Label the hot and cold water faucets.
- Turn water temperature to 120° F.
- Have him wear an identification tag on a necklace or bracelet so that he can be identified if he becomes lost. Include on the tag his name, your name, and phone numbers where you can be contacted.
- Install handrails and grab bars where needed throughout the house to minimize the risk of falls.
- Keep hazardous cleaners, medicines, matches, and other potentially dangerous items out of reach. Think back to when you childproofed your home and do it again.
- Make sure all doors to the outside are locked at night. Install an alarm so that when doors are open you'll hear and know that your relative may be trying to go out unattended.
- Seek safety stove tips from your electrician. Remove stove knobs when you're not around to supervise the use of the stove.

Dementia often brings out the worst in a caregiver. It's like taking care of a stranger at times, and the emotional connection that you had with the person is often lost under a haze of confusion, mood swings, and forgetfulness. It's hard to hold on to good feelings when the person you love is screaming at you or looking at you as if they have forgotten who you are. Hold on to your good memories. Look at it as if they have made deposits in your emotional bank and are now making withdrawals.

Unfortunately, it's easy to get in a pattern of yelling back or otherwise being emotionally abusive. Physical abuse of the person with dementia is not uncommon. To make sure that you don't find yourself in this type of tragic situation, take the time to talk about your feelings of anger, resentment, disappointment, and frustration to someone who supports you. This person could be your spouse, clergyman, mental health professional, or friend. It can be someone who has gone through the same type of ordeal. You don't want to get caught in a destructive pattern of behavior. Remember, the more out of control you are, the harder it will be for your relative—a person who is already confused and having a hard time managing.

Family members of relatives who suffer from dementia report that there are usually fleeting moments of normalcy in their relative's behavior and conversation. There are brief moments in the day when their relative seems like his or her old self. Cherish these moments. Laugh, hug, talk, touch, and most of all enjoy these moments.

Remind yourself that the odd behaviors, the frequent change in mood, the deterioration in ability to function are part of the illness of dementia. Your parent or relative is not behaving this way on purpose or out of a desire to make your life difficult.

Join a support group to talk about your feelings. You are living through a period in which you are losing your parent. To help your parent, make a plan for each day and stick to it. Individuals with dementia often find it difficult to adjust to changes in their daily routine. If you take your relative to a day-care program, help her settle into routine gradually. If home care is the option you've chosen, try to arrange for the worker to come when you're home and gradually increase the amount of time she is left with the worker.

Because it's easier to care for someone when you know exactly what they need and like, provide the home care worker with detailed instructions. Include a list of problems that sometimes occur and the solutions you've come up with to resolve them.

MEMORY LOSS

Tips to Help Those Suffering from Memory Loss

Coping with loss of memory is difficult for both the caregiver and the recipient of care. Memory loss is frightening, confusing, and embarrassing. To help those who have experienced memory loss, caregivers should do the following:

- Provide as much consistency as possible in the home.
- Pprovide as much structure as possible in the daily routine. For example, schedule mealtimes for the same time each day. Don't vary your relative's schedule too much.
- Leave written notes wherever necessary throughout the house to help your loved one function on a day-to-day basis.
- Place emergency phone numbers, daily schedules, and information that helps your loved one reorient herself when she becomes confused. For example, "Today is Thursday. The bus will come to take you to the day-care center. Joy, the home health aide, will help you get on the bus. Your daughter will be home waiting for you when the bus brings you back."

- Minimize the changes that occur in your home. For example, don't move the furniture to different positions frequently. Keep your loved one's possessions in one place and don't vary it. Dentures, eyeglasses, and canes should be placed in the same location when they are taken out or off.

PHYSICAL PROBLEMS

Changes in behavior are sometimes a sign of an underlying physical problem. For example, if your parent is suffering from loss of vision, he may react by losing interest in going places or doing activities that he would typically want to do. He may appear withdrawn. He might not realize that his vision has become impaired. He just knows that something isn't right. Schedule regular checkups with an ophthalmologist. Have annual checks for glaucoma. Maintain proper care of other health conditions that can cause vision problems, such as diabetes.

Hearing loss is another common problem among the elderly. Problems with hearing can lead to depression, confusion, paranoid behavior, and disorientation. When you can't hear those who are talking near you, it's common to think that everyone's whispering. Sometimes it seems that because you can't hear them they must not want to be heard because they're talking about you. Hearing problems lead to social withdrawal and social isolation.

NUTRITIONAL PROBLEMS

Nutritional problems are common among the elderly. Those who live alone often stop eating regularly due to disinterest in eating alone or to difficulty cooking or preparing meals. Digestion is often difficult due to dental problems or muscle problems. Medications can sometimes cause foods to taste strange. Illness can also contribute to loss of appetite. As we age, the sensitivity of our taste buds decreases, limiting our ability to perceive the actual taste of the food we're eating. Changes in our sense of smell also contribute to difficulty enjoying food. We discuss using a nutritional program in Chapter 17. However, caregivers can do many things to help their relatives continue to eat balanced, nutritional, and enjoyable meals.

First of all, we usually enjoy meals more when we eat with others. So encourage your loved one to join the family at mealtime. Stimulating conversation can provide a boost to the appetite. Even listening to an "argument" about whose turn it is to load the dishwasher can be better than eating alone. Your loved one is also likely to eat because she's sitting at the table longer than she would if she were alone.

When preparing meals, adhere to special dietary needs and encourage your loved one to accept the changes in diet that have been recommended by the physician.

If your loved one is having difficulty sleeping, and her physician has ruled out a physiological cause, try offering her warm milk at bedtime. Ask if she'd like soft music played in her room. Sometimes feelings of anxiety or depression cause difficulty sleeping and eating. Counseling with a mental health professional trained in geriatric care can also be helpful. Medication is sometimes prescribed for these problems by an internist or psychiatrist. Remember to coordinate all parts of your relative's medical care so that she is not overmedicated.

Your loved one's primary care physician should be kept informed of all problems and conditions. The physician should know about all treatments that are rendered and the medications that are prescribed. Remember that elderly people respond differently than younger people to medication.

MEDICATION PROBLEMS AMONG THE ELDERLY

For elderly people, medications are often prescribed for conditions such as hypertension, diabetes, arthritis, cardiopulmonary disorders, depression, and anxiety. However, many elderly people don't take their medication correctly, and there are many reasons for this. By knowing the warning signs of noncompliance, the caregiver can ensure that their relative receives proper care.

Noncompliance can take different forms. Sometimes too much medication is taken, whereas other times too little medication is taken. These types of mistakes are usually not done on purpose. However, when someone purposely doesn't take the right amount of medicine or doesn't take it at all, it's often because he or she doesn't like some part of the prescribed regimen.

For example, she may dislike the side effects, the type or amount of medicine prescribed, or the necessity of taking the medicine at a particular time. Feelings of anxiety about taking the medicine can also cause noncompliance. Being informed that you have an illness or condition that needs medical care is itself anxiety provoking. Sometimes it's hard to take in all the information the doctor is telling you at that moment.

Vision and hearing problems are two other causes of noncompliance. Memory loss and a tendency to be forgetful also contribute to noncompliance. Researchers have found that elderly people who live alone and become socially isolated are less likely to comply with prescribed care (Haynes et al. 1980). There is also a strong correlation between the number of medicines prescribed and compliance. The greater the number of prescriptions the less likely the patient is to comply with the prescribed care routine (Darnell et al. 1986).

Sometimes the elderly person does not clearly understand the physician's instructions. Like many people, instead of asking questions to clarify his confusion, he just doesn't take the medicine.

Tips to increase compliance with taking medication:

- Develop a good patient–physician relationship. Seek a doctor who is trained in caring for elderly people. Go with your loved one to their appointments and listen closely to how they communicate with one another. Does the doctor speak to her in a clear, understandable manner? Does he attempt to motivate your loved one to act in her own best interests?
- To reduce confusion about which medicine to take and when to take it, write the name of the drug and the reason for taking it on the container. Write in large, easily visible letters.
- To help with memory loss, repeat instructions periodically. Talk with your loved one in a nonconfrontational manner to see if she understands when she's supposed to take her medicine.
- Leave patient package inserts in view to reinforce verbal instructions.
- Use containers that do not have childproof caps (unless, due to your relative's mental state, this would place her at risk).
- Pill sorters help minimize confusion about taking medicine. Sorters are available in most pharmacies and supermarkets.

Studies have shown that there is greater compliance when the patient's family supports the prescribed care regimen. This finding is most likely a result of the tendency for supportive families to be willing to supervise the use of the medication (Shaw and Opit, 1976; Haynes, 1976).

A NOTE TO THE SPOUSE OF THE CAREGIVER

With your blessing, and after many discussions, your wife's mother has moved into your home after suffering a stroke. She was widowed many years ago, so there's no one else who can help her recuperate. The plan is for her to stay in your home for at least a few months. But you and your wife have talked about the possibility that your mother-in-law will never live on her own again.

You probably didn't realize how big a change this would cause in your life. You can be certain that your wife didn't know either. So hang in there and work this out together. Tackle problems and chores as a team.

For example, when you see your wife putting up with her mother's crankiness, resist the impulse to get angry at your wife or your mother-in-law. This is probably not the first time this has happened between them. Not that your wife likes it. But right now, with all the stress she's feeling, she could use your support in dealing with her mother.

Help your wife respond in a way that lets her mother know that her behavior is hurtful. Let her know that in your home, that kind of talk is unacceptable. Although you may not be able to change the behavior, you'll ease her stress by supporting her and letting her know that you understand her feelings and see how difficult this situation is for her. This can strengthen your marital relationship.

The Following List Describes Ways to Help Your Caregiver Spouse

- Pay attention to her needs.
- Take time to be alone with each other.
- Fulfill your promises. If you said you'd help by keeping track of her mother's appointments, do it.
- Recognize when you need a "time out"—take a break.

- Recognize when your wife needs a "time out"—encourage her to take time for herself.
- Get to know the support network of family and friends who've agreed to help. Acknowledge their usefulness.
- Don't stop communicating with your spouse; pay attention to your relationship.
- Separate caregiver problems from marital or family problems.
- Join a support group. This will develop your awareness of what your spouse is going through, and you'll meet other spouses who, like you, are providing a home for their spouse's parent.
- If you can't resolve conflicts together, seek professional counseling.

TAKING CARE OF YOUR SPOUSE

You've both worked hard all of your life. The children are grown, and they live on their own. Now you've both retired. All's well. Then your husband gets sick. This is not the way you'd pictured your retirement years with your loved one. You've saved money in anticipation of traveling together or spending your days having fun.

Then your husband had a stroke. Luckily, he is recuperating and has been discharged from the hospital. Now what are you supposed to do? How are you supposed to feel? Your life has veered off course in a new direction.

You've made the decision to hire health care workers to come to your home and provide care to your husband. But there are many tasks you will undertake on your own.

For example, he needs help shaving and bathing in the morning. So you've started getting up an hour earlier to have your coffee before he awakens and needs you. You still play bridge with your friends every Wednesday, but now you rush home feeling tense, because you know he likes you to be home with him. You feel nervous about leaving him alone with the visiting nurse. She's competent and professional, but he's not accustomed to her yet.

His doctor says he's getting better, and his physical condition does seem to be improving. But, to you, he doesn't seem to be the same person he used to be before getting sick. You find yourself unable to sleep at night because you're worried about him, worried about yourself, worried about everything. Some days you feel exhausted. Other days you think that nothing will ever be the same. You notice that your friends don't come over on the spur of the moment as they used to. You start feeling lonely, angry, and frightened.

Friends, family members, and doctors all focus on your husband, and no one notices that you're distressed. After all, you've suffered many losses.

- You've lost your husband, as he once was.
- You've lost the feeling of assurance that all is well.
- You've lost the freedom to do what you want when you want.
- You've lost the feeling of financial security. You've had to spend a lot of money on his care, and you worry about the long-term effect of this on your financial security.

If, in general, you've had a good marital relationship, then you have a foundation on which to build the blocks of a new phase of your relationship. But even in the best of relationships, change is difficult. Roles in the marital relationship will change out of necessity.

When a wife becomes a caregiver, she may have to assume a role that she has moved away from during the course of the marriage. Her children are now less dependent on her. She may have started or developed her career. She may have been looking forward to enjoying this phase of her life in which she no longer has an obligation to take care of anyone. She now has to adjust to providing for her husband's physical comfort and care. Or, she may have relied on her husband to make household repairs and manage their finances—responsibilities which he can no longer take care of for her. She now has to pay bills, hire someone to cut the lawn and clean the gutters, and make sure the car is on a maintenance schedule. The list is endless. The point is that sometimes we get what we haven't asked for from life. The task is then to figure out how to adjust and make the most of it.

When a husband becomes his wife's caregiver, an even greater change occurs. Typically, men in our society have not held the role of primary caregiver. Their ability to physically take care of others may be rusty. They may need coaching to learn to cook, clean, and help their wife take a bath. The husband may not be accustomed to doing these tasks. Although he may not object to doing them, he may be reluctant to ask others for help. At such times, support from the couple's children and friends can make a positive difference.

But, so far, we've only looked at the external changes that occur. How about the feelings that each person is experiencing? It's likely that the spouse who needs help is feeling many strong, often conflicting emotions. He may feel embarrassed about his loss of physical strength or about his inability to take care of his wife the way he used to. He may have highly valued his privacy in the past, but now that he needs help going to the bathroom and changing his bandages, he can't have the same amount of privacy. He might also feel conflicted about the attention and care he receives. He needs help, but he doesn't want to need it. He feels frustrated, and in his frustration, he might lash out at the very person who is helping him—his wife.

The caregiver also has conflicting feelings. She wants to help her husband and she wants him to get better. But she's tired and overwhelmed and when he acts irritable or ill-tempered, she feels angry and resentful. Neither of you wants things to be the way they are.

The couple's personal boundaries may have to change. Along with this change in the amount of personal space comes a change in the relationship. For example, changes in the way one looks, due to surgery, for example, may cause one spouse to avoid intimacy. The ill spouse has to cope with changes in health, the changes in the way his or her body looks and, possibly, the injury to self-esteem caused by these changes.

The spouse and a strong support system can help her regain a positive outlook and to feel better about herself. Members of the support system should be sensitive to changes in her mood and overall functioning and encourage her to seek professional help if she becomes depressed or unable to function.

In the best of circumstances, conflict can be resolved by expressing your feelings and expectations. However, caregivers whose spouses suffer from dementia or other cognitive impairment probably won't get relief by talking it over with their loved one. They should seek help from support groups or trained mental health professionals. The Appendix lists the names and phone numbers of support groups. Organizations such as the Well Spouse Foundation are proof of the need for healthy spouses to receive support from others who are in a similar situation.

TAKING CARE OF YOUR PARTNER—CAREGIVERS IN UNTRADITIONAL FAMILIES

Couples who have lived together but are not legally married and couples in gay or lesbian relationships often face all the caregiver problems of those in more traditional households as well as many other problems.

In gay or lesbian relationships, the family members of the ill or disabled person who now needs care may refuse to acknowledge the partner's role in their loved one's life. This can have major consequences since important decisions have to be made about care. Family members often don't consult the partner and, instead, fail to acknowledge their presence or behave as though their presence is unimportant. They are ignoring their loved one's wishes, which is likely to have a negative impact on his well-being and recovery.

Family members are not the only ones to ignore the partner in these relationships. You could be refused medical information by health care practitioners until a "blood" relative is present. You can take steps to protect yourself and your loved one before these kinds of problems arise.

There are legal documents that you can execute, such as medical proxies (which are discussed in Chapter 22) to ensure that this doesn't happen.

We've discussed some of the problems that can arise for couples in nontraditional relationships. The strengths that exist in these relationships often become evident when problems occur. For instance, couples who have lived together in a lifestyle objected to by others often develop a bond that unifies them against the disapproving members of the outside world. As a result, they may have already developed the ability to cope on their own. Still, as with most caregivers, they'll find it beneficial to develop and maintain a network of people who support their relationship and who are willing to help with the responsibilities of caregiving.

THE SIBLING RELATIONSHIP AND CAREGIVING

In the best of all circumstances, your brothers or sisters are willing to help you care for your parent. Together, you've worked out a viable plan in which you each share part of the responsibility for care and everyone pitches in and does what they've promised to do. When problems arise, you're able to work it out to everyone's satisfaction.

Unfortunately, it doesn't always work this way. Sometimes, siblings strongly disagree with each other about how to care for their parent. For example, Tom's seventy-year-old-mother suffered a massive stroke. After the hospital discharged her, he decided not to place her in a nursing home even though this was affordable because she had saved plenty of money. He thinks that his mother will be just fine at home with a hired companion and occasional visits from the nurse. You, Tom's sister, want your mother to receive the best care available. You think to yourself, "How dare Tom presume to know what's best for Mother?" But Tom has been appointed in charge of her finances. What can you do?

Set aside your feelings about Tom and focus on Mother. Talk with Tom about Mother's needs. Say, "Mother looks depressed. She's accustomed to seeing friends and being active. Now that she is all alone, she's withdrawing more each day. She needs physical therapy and intellectual stimulation."

Don't say, "I want Mother to be placed in a home where she can have the therapy she needs. . ." You may have to discuss this problem with Tom many times before he becomes willing to give it a try. Or you may have to seek out community services such as volunteers to come visit your mother.

Another option is to talk with Tom and see if he'll agree to move Mother into a nursing home on a trial basis. Specify the changes in her level of functioning or demeanor that will be used as an indicator of whether the nursing home placement was a good decision. Ask Tom to take a close look at Mother before she goes into the nursing home and then to compare it to how she seems in about six months after she's been there. It takes most elderly people about this much time to fully adjust to changes in their environment.

Consult a physician trained in geriatrics and request a meeting with him, your mother, and Tom. The physician can validate your view and inform Tom about whether placement in a nursing home is a good idea at this time.

The Only Child

Having siblings can make caregiving complicated, but being an only child has unique pluses and minuses. Although you can make the decisions you want regarding your parent's care, there are no siblings with whom you can share the responsibility, fears, and anxieties about your decisions. You may have a supportive spouse or partner, but sometimes they resent the time and energy necessary to perform the caregiving duties. Like many only children, you may have already built strong relationships with friends, cousins, and other relatives. You're likely to find others your age who are going through similar problems related to caregiving. Use whatever support is available. You can also join a support group.

PROVIDING CARE FROM A DISTANCE

Although caring for a relative who lives with you can be difficult, caregiving from a distance has its own set of problems. It's estimated that six million Americans care for relatives from a distance. You may not know all of the resources available in your relative's community. You may find yourself often worrying about them because you aren't able to see for yourself how they are doing. You may doubt that they are doing as well as they tell you they are. Visit them to determine their network of friends or family who are willing to help them in your absence or to determine who you can call on in case of emergency.

Consider hiring a geriatric care manager so that services can be coordinated and maintained. Plan to speak with the care manager regularly so that you can stay informed of any potential problems or changes that need to be made.

Care comes in many packages, depending on the needs and abilities of the individual. For example, your relative may need in-home medical care, community-based services, or help with managing at home during recovery from an illness. In order to figure out what your relative needs, you need to properly assess his or her capabilities. While you may be able to do this on your own, you may get a more comprehensive, realistic assessment if you get help from your relatives' physician or a geriatric care manager.

The care manager is usually a nurse or a social worker with a master's degree who has expertise in evaluating needs to determine what services are needed.

The care manager also monitors the care provided and re-assesses the plan regularly to ensure that it continues to meet the individual's needs.

Care managers are particularly helpful when many services need to be coordinated with one another. You will want your care manager to be aware of the resources available in your relative's community.

For those family members who are trying to take care of a relative from a distance, a care manager can be the answer to your prayers. When problems arise, you do not have to take time off from work and miss your child's school play in order to hop on a plane and find out what has gone wrong. Call the care manager and schedule a time to talk on the phone about the problem. You will want a care manager with whom you can communicate as well as one who communicates well with your relative. Do not lose sight of the fact that even with a care manager in the picture, your relative's input is always important. Interventions and treatments will not help if the recipient of the care has a strong objection to or anxiety about the plan.

Care management services provided through Medicaid or your long-term care insurance company are usually provided at no cost. The cost of care management services provided through a state or local governmental agency may be based on your income or may be free. Private care managers cost between $100 and $150 per hour.

During your meeting with the care manager, your relative's eligibility will be determined. An assessment of needs will be done. Services will be set up and care will be monitored on an ongoing basis. You will need to have the following documents available:

- health and disability insurance policies;
- long-term care insurance policies;
- military discharge papers;
- living will (medical directive);
- checking and savings account information;
- pension documents;
- a list of all current prescription and over-the-counter medications; and
- the names of physicians, therapists, etc. who are presently involved in care (include full name, specialty, telephone number and address).

The National Case Management Partnership is a nonprofit network of more than two hundred case management agencies in the United States. You can contact them for information or contact the Area Agency on Aging. Or contact your hospital's department of social work or discharge planning. The National Association of Private Geriatric Care Managers is an organization that can refer you to geriatric care managers in your area. (See Appendix.)

Even if you've hired a care manager, you'll probably want to keep track of your parents' appointments so that you can be sure they're getting the care they need. Get a calendar or an appointment book and use it only for this purpose. Make notes on it to yourself if you plan to call in advance to remind them about the appointment or if you want to call them after the appointment to see how well it went.

If your parent has difficulty remembering to take care of household business or pay bills on time, you can have the bills mailed directly to you. After signing the necessary documents at her bank, you can be allowed access to her account to write checks on her behalf.

In addition to hiring a geriatric care manager, it's easier to be a long-distance caregiver if you do the following things:

- Develop a network of family and friends in your parent's neighborhood who can help her and whom you can contact in case of an emergency.
- Make appointments with those who are providing care to her *before* you plan to travel to her town. It's unfair to expect the social worker or your mother's physician to be able to schedule an appointment to meet with you on short notice. By scheduling in advance, you can get the most out of your efforts to coordinate her care and make sure there are no problems.
- Consider purchasing an emergency response or alert system for your parent's home.
- Give a spare key to your parent's house to one of her trusted neighbors. This way she can gain access in case of an emergency.
- Use the community services that are available in your parent's neighborhood, such as elder watch programs or Meals On Wheels.

PART THREE

An In-Depth Look at What's Available

11

Nursing Home Care

MAKING THE CHOICE

One of the hardest things you'll ever have to do is to put Mom in a nursing home. We see ourselves in her, and we worry about how we would feel if this happened to us. Most of us get great pleasure from the sense of freedom and control that comes from living on our own in our house or apartment. The thought of having to live otherwise is frightening. It is anathema to our sense of being adults. Yet, independent living is no longer possible when we require significant assistance to care for ourselves or when our medical condition warrants routine monitoring or assistance.

Likewise, for other reasons, family members often find it hard to make the decision to place a relative in a nursing home. They feel as though they are abandoning their elderly loved one or that they are admitting defeat about their ability to take care of their loved one. The elderly relative may try to make you feel that you are a bad person for making this choice.

While you may know *intellectually* that you cannot physically take care of your family member, emotionally this fact can be hard to accept. Some parents clearly state their expectations about what they think their children should do for them. Often, these same parents have difficulty recognizing the stress you feel as you attempt to manage your life and theirs. Such relatives usually become noticeably demanding after their spouses die, often making it necessary for them to have other relatives help fulfill their needs.

Support groups can help you deal with the conflict you may feel once you've made the decision to place a relative in a nursing home. Support group members can help you recognize the realities and problems you faced when you tried in other ways to provide care. After all, the decision to place a relative in a nursing home is rarely made quickly. Typically, other arrangements have been tried first and failed. Even your elderly relative, who initially may have been reluctant to move into a nursing home, may change his view once he experiences firsthand that he receives better care in the nursing home than he was able to provide for himself or to receive from you.

In the most difficult of circumstances, the decision to move a relative into a nursing home follows a crisis situation, such as after discharge from the hospital. At other times, the move is made when the caregiver becomes ill or can no longer handle the responsibilities involved in providing care. Nursing homes also become an option when spouses are too ill to care for each other as they once did. In the best of circumstances, this move is made after much planning and research.

It's helpful to encourage your relative's participation in determining which nursing home is suitable. It is important to recognize that this is a major change in lifestyle and that, emotionally, it represents another significant phase of life. Your relative may be extremely reluctant to give up the independence that comes from living on his own, even though he needs a great deal of assistance. Even if he doesn't talk about these feelings with you, raise the topic yourself. Open communication about his fears and worries can help smooth the process for everyone. Once he realizes that you do not intend to drop him off at the door of the nursing home and never return, he may be more willing to participate in the process of thinking about making the change to a nursing home.

There are many advantages to living in a nursing home. Help them focus on these factors. For example, they will have access to activities and social gatherings that they may previously have been unable to attend due to transportation problems. They will also have an opportunity to meet new people who are their age and who share their interests. Many elderly people are reluctant or disinterested in meeting new people because of the many friends they've lost. Understandably, many elderly people are not enthusiastic about starting new friendships. However, with understanding and encouragement, many elderly people become willing to improve their lives by letting new people and new experiences in.

Everyone involved will need time to adjust to this change. It will take time for your relative to get used to the nursing home.

There are things you can do to help them during this time.

- If at all possible, do not sell their home right away.
- If finances permit, give them time to become accustomed to their new residence before doing away with the previous one. As a result, they are not faced with closing one door in their lives before they have opened the next door. In addition, they will not have to throw out or give away their personal belongings at the same time that they are having to adjust to a new environment and to the many changes in their daily routine.

Imagine how you'd feel if you had to sell your possessions, close up your house and move into a much smaller living space, and leave the friends and a neighborhood you loved—all at the same time. To many people, these changes signal the final phase of their life and that realization can bring on a strong, almost overwhelming sense of loss.

Continued attention and care from family members and friends helps tremendously. Visit and call your loved one regularly. Many people visit on the same day each week so that their relative knows when to expect you and can anticipate the visit. This way they do not have to worry that if they are busy elsewhere in the nursing home they may miss your visit.

Staff in the home will recognize that your relative is cared by your family, and this may make them more responsive to the needs of your family member. Visits from friends and neighbors also help your relative to not feel abandoned. It is also important to maintain a connection to the outside world. Others adjust best by focusing only on the routine of the nursing home. The daily menu, the residents, and the schedule become their main focus.

The adjustment to having a family member living in a nursing home can be stressful for all family members. While you may feel a huge sense of relief, you may also worry about whether you chose the right home and whether your relative will be well cared for. Remember that as with most major changes, adjustment is a gradual process. Your relative's initial reaction may be negative, and he or she may be resistant to adapting to the new environment, but this does not mean that they will not eventually be glad they are there.

In many nursing homes, residents share a room with another resident. This is a big change for most people which requires a great deal of adjustment. Many people have never lived with a stranger; others may not have done so since their college years. This transition will certainly take time. Place personal belongings in their room to make it cozy and familiar. Talk with your relative about what pictures or books they want. Use caution when deciding about valuables, because theft often occurs. Talk with your relative to make a plan about valuable items they want to see often, but which would not be safe if left in the home. For example, jewelry and other valuable mementos have sentimental and monetary value and are an important link to the person's past. However, jewelry may be stolen. Perhaps you can bring them to the nursing home in a keepsake box when you visit. Before moving in, make a list of your relative's possessions. Print their name in each article of clothing and in the bottom of other possessions.

Help your relative maintain interest in the world around them by reading to them, listening to music with them, helping them write letters or composing audio messages for friends and family members. Take them out if possible, for a walk or to their church, or to visit a friend. Drive one of their friends to the nursing home to visit them. Remember to show them that you care about them and are not abandoning them. Continue to touch them. If they are already bathed when you visit, offer to give them a manicure or brush their hair, or apply their favorite lotion.

Help them to become involved in the activities that are offered. Encourage them to help others around them so as not to become preoccupied with themselves. Remember that often when a bed becomes available in a nursing home it is because the resident has died. Their roommate needs time to adjust to this loss as well as to get used to living with someone new. These types of changes cause feelings of loss to be stirred up and, once again, there is an adjustment to be made.

Many nursing homes offer exercise classes, rehabilitative therapy, and social activities. Let your loved one know how well they are doing in getting accustomed to their new surroundings. Praise even their smallest attempt to get involved.

The atmosphere in a nursing home is very different from that in a private home. For example, there is a set time for most activities, including eating, activities, and dispensing of medication. We all enjoy setting up our own routines. We like to decide when we want to have our first cup of coffee for the day or when we want to read the newspaper.

Residents may feel a loss of control over aspects of their lives they could previously control. This is hard for family members as well. You may have to wait until a staff member dispenses medication for pain or to help one go to sleep. In your own home, you could decide when to take the medication. Family members should be an advocate for their relatives, speaking diplomatically to nursing home staff to determine how to resolve this problem.

CHOOSING A NURSING HOME

The thought of trying to choose a good nursing home can make you feel anxious. There are many aspects to consider in your decision, including quality of care, location, cost, and eligibility. Newspapers often report abuses that occur in nursing homes, and this is everyone's worst fear. The Nursing Home Quality Reform law was enacted in 1987 to address in part these problems. Since this law has been enacted, it is reported that the use of physical restraints has declined by more than 40 percent, detection and resolution of abuse has improved tenfold, and the need for hospitalization of residents has declined by 25 percent (AARP). As stated in this law, a nursing home must take into consideration an individual's needs and preferences so as to preserve their quality of life. In this context, both the psychological and the physical well-being of the resident must be nurtured. Nursing home residents should expect to be treated with dignity and respect. They should be given reasonable opportunity to make decisions about aspects of their daily lives. Staff should interact with residents in a caring and courteous manner.

The emotional state of people who are treated without respect or consideration for their needs declines rapidly. The elderly are particularly prone to becoming confused or withdrawn when their needs are unmet. Depression can develop or worsen as the person's identity is ignored, causing them to lose a sense of self.

Under Federal law, residents have various rights, including the right of privacy in care and confidentiality regarding their personal, medical, and financial matters. They have the right to have their possessions secured against theft. They have the right to be protected against transfer unless for specific reasons. We will discuss some of these rights in this section. You can request a full list of residents' rights called The Bill of Rights.

First of all, it is important to know that residents have the right to participate in planning the care they will receive. This means that they are to be fully informed of any decisions about treatment and that they should participate in the decision-making process. If the resident is unable to do this due to medical or mental incapacity, their family member or legal representative should be involved on their behalf. The resident has the right to refuse treatment and receive information about appropriate alternatives. They ought to be able to administer their own medication unless it has been determined that this is unsafe for them.

Residents also have the right to exercise choice in matters such as when to get up and go to bed, what clothing to wear, and deciding which activities they want to participate in. They also have the right to snacks outside of regularly scheduled meals and should receive a choice from main meals. They have the right to associate with whom they choose, which includes the right to share a room with a spouse and the right to gather with any of the residents without a staff person present. They have the right to privacy.

When considering resident's rights to optimal care, the issue of the use of restraints arises. Until recently, restraints were a common way to control or manage nursing home residents. Physical restraints such as vests, wrist and waist restraints, hand mitts, or chairs with table trays were often used. Chemical restraints such as psychoactive drugs were also used.

There are many obvious drawbacks to the use of restraints. Physical restraints can cause symptoms that have underlying causes to go undetected. Instead of solving a problem, restraints mask the problem and prevent the resident from being able to express his or her needs or distress. Residents who are physically restrained tend to become agitated or depressed. Some people resort to screaming, whereas others lapse into a state of depression or withdrawal. Those are the devastating emotional effects of restraint use. The physical effects are incontinence, dehydration, and swollen feet and ankles from sitting in one place for too long, and pneumonia from not moving for long periods of time.

Chemical restraints are also used to control behaviors such as difficulty sleeping, depression, and anxiety attacks. These behaviors all have underlying causes and should first be treated with other methods. Ask the staff what types of treatment have been attempted:

- For the resident who cannot sleep—have staff tried to find out what has caused this sudden change? Have they attempted to offer a warm bath or a glass of hot milk?
- For the resident who is depressed—has there been a loss or a major change in life?
- Have they encouraged him to talk or write about what is bothering him?
- Is he in physical pain?
- Has he been prescribed a type of medication that is causing him to feel depressed?

In advocating for your relative, if the use of restraints has been recommended, you should ask the following questions.

- What symptom led to the use of a restraint?
- Has the cause of the symptom been properly assessed?
- What efforts have staff members made to treat or alleviate the cause?
- Has anyone given attention to the individual's needs or habits?
- Has his routine in some way been disrupted?
- Is the person developing an infection or illness?
- Is he having difficulty communicating his distress?
- What is the plan for discontinuance of restraint?

Schedule an appointment to speak to your relative's physician to find out what else can be done. Psychotherapy sessions can help the elderly resolve feelings about the losses they have experienced.

The following list provides conditions or situations under which the nursing home is allowed to transfer your loved one to another facility.

- If by remaining in the home, their health would be endangered.

- If a bill has not been paid after sufficient notice has been given and a reasonable amount of time has elapsed.
- When the resident's needs cannot be met in that facility.
- When the resident no longer needs to remain, due to improvement in health.

However, the facility must notify the resident, the family or their legal representative in writing before they can transfer the resident. Notification must include: (1) the specific reasons for the intended move, (2) a statement that informs that the resident has the right to appeal, (3) thirty days notice of the plan to move the resident, and (4) the name, address, and telephone number of the state long-term care ombudsman. Residents may refuse to be transferred if the move is based on Medicaid eligibility. In this case, they are entitled to a hearing.

When residents are transferred to a hospital, the nursing home must give the resident and the family written notice about how long the bed will be reserved and whether there is any fee charged for their bed to be held for them until they return.

Nursing homes can be non profit, such as those sponsored by religious organizations. However, most nursing homes are private enterprises operated by their owners primarily—or solely—to earn a profit.

Most states have two licensing levels—intermediate and skilled—based on the residents' physical and mental capabilities and needs. Residents are often situated in the home according to the level of care needed. Those who are less disabled are then not faced with exposure to those who are disabled or seriously ill. This can help them emotionally, because we all fear getting ill and dying and can become frightened and anxious when those around us are ill or dying.

In addition to financial considerations, location of the home is important. Preferably, the home should be near family and friends so that they can visit. If the spouse of a nursing home resident will need to use public transportation to visit, the home should be located near public transportation.

Appearance of the home is also important. The exterior of the nursing home should have areas for the residents to sit or walk. This area should be clean, well-lit, and free of obstacles. Check to make sure that the food is nutritious and tastes good. You don't want your relative skipping meals or depending on visitors to bring food in order to maintain a healthy diet. Residents who need help with eating should be given it in a courteous manner. Those who have special dietary needs should have these meals available.

A variety of activities should be offered, and the curriculum should meet one's physical, emotional, intellectual, and spiritual needs. Activities should be posted where all residents can see them. Because the residents have differing capabilities, these should be considered and reflected in the types of activities offered. For example, those who have trouble talking or singing may want to join in and listen to those who can sing, and they should be allowed to do so in comfort. Those who want challenging crossword puzzles should have access to them, whereas those who want less challenging mental stimulation should also have this available to them.

It's a good sign when volunteers are involved in the daily routine of the nursing home because more care and attention can be given to each resident. You also need to make sure that residents have access to telephones and that they have privacy when needed. Visitors should be made to feel welcomed. Residents should be assigned to rooms with thought given to their level of care needed and their disabilities, abilities, interests, and personalities. It's not a good sign if Mr. R is assigned to room with Mr. G when it's a known fact that Mr. R is a night owl and Mr. G gets up at dawn.

You and your family members naturally will be concerned about the staff of the nursing home. The staff–resident ratio is important so that quality of care can be maintained and staff are not overworked. Before making a decision about placing your relative in a nursing home, visit during the day and at night to see the changes that occur when staffing shifts change. Take note of the interaction between staff and residents.

- Does the staff talk to the residents?
- Is staff pleasant and courteous to the residents?
- Does staff touch the residents when appropriate or necessary?
- Does staff seem appropriately caring?

The costs of all services should be available and should be written and itemized. Don't assume that everything is included when you are quoted a price about a particular service. Request an admissions contract. Get written information about what happens when the source of payment changes from private pay to Medicaid.

Determine what services are offered in the home. Get written information about specific services.

- Are rehabilitation therapies available?
- Is the equipment up to date, clean, and in proper working condition?
- How often is a registered physical therapist present? Often, physical therapy aides are used, and the registered physical therapist is used mainly for supervision and consultation.
- Is a social worker present?
- Does the home require the use of an in-home physician? If so, your physician's orders will be in the domain of the nursing home physician. This could affect continuity of care, medication, and treatment.
- What is the nursing home's policy on visits, personal belongings, food, and gifts?
- Can visitors bring food for their relative? How is it stored?
- Is individuality encouraged?
- Are religious services offered?
- Will your relative receive enough intellectual stimulation?
- Are staff assigned to work with the same residents on a consistent basis? This is helpful because then the workers learn the individual needs of the residents and can help them recognize when there is a problem. In addition, the residents can then become accustomed to seeing the same faces and can begin to trust that their needs will be understood and met.

PLANNING FOR CARE IN A NURSING HOME

Each resident must have an individualized plan of care. The plan should state what each staff person will do with or for your relative and when they are to do it. This information is determined in a case planning conference. Your relative and you or another family member should be present during this conference. Other people that should be present at the conference include the personal physician, a nurse, social worker, nursing assistants, pharmacists, therapists, and any other nursing home staff who will be responsible for providing direct care to your relative. This part of the process can help your relative adjust to the nursing home. It is an opportunity for her needs to be heard and for a plan to be devised in order to make her comfortable and to improve her ability to function or otherwise improve her health.

Nursing home conditions are monitored periodically using surveys. These are inspections of various aspects of the residence. However, because the surveys are only done periodically, it is important for the families of the residents to advocate on their behalf and ensure that the conditions remain safe and comfortable.

There are times when despite all of your work, problems still arise, and you are displeased about some aspect of care. Before moving your relative from the nursing home, make sure that you have done all you can to change the condition that you found unacceptable. This can be done in a number of ways. You or your relative's legal representative has the right to meet with nursing home staff to discuss the care plan as well as any problems that arise once your relative has started to live there. First talk with the staff about the problem. If one of your relative's possessions is missing, send a letter asking that the item be located. Include a date by which you expect to hear from the nursing director—be reasonable. Inquire about the nursing home's policy for replacing lost possessions. Many home insurance policies can be amended to include your relative's belongings.

If the care plan seems problematic, ask to arrange another care planning meeting. Be specific about the problem. Focus on solving the problem and state the specific changes you want to see in order to know that the problem has been solved. Ask other residents in the home to see if they are having the same problem. You should keep a record of when the problem occurs and which staff member is on duty during that time. It is also important to make note of who you spoke to about the problem and what type of solutions were attempted. After meeting about the problem, send a written summary of what was decided to the director so that there is clear communication and documentation of what transpired.

If that doesn't work, ask the long-term care ombudsman for assistance. The ombudsman's job is to investigate and attempt to resolve problems or complaints. An ombudsman is assigned to advocate for every nursing home. Each state has a long-term care ombudsman who can tell you who to contact for problems in the nursing home that you are concerned about.

Nursing homes also have organized resident councils and family or community councils. The resident councils meet regularly to discuss and make recommendations about the policies of the nursing homes.

Although family councils usually provide support, some act as advocates for the residents, seeking changes in policy and care.

You can also file a formal complaint with the board that licenses or certifies any health care worker with whom you may be having a problem. Every state has a particular agency, usually functioning within the Department of Health, whose job it is to resolve complaints about the various health care workers.

Don't get so caught up in the problem-solving effort that you forget to respect the rights of your relative. Your actions can affect the care that is provided. Begin by trying to establish a working relationship with staff. Support your relative's dignity and rights and expect the staff to do the same. Know your rights and the rights of the resident. You should advocate with the goal of finding solutions, not placing blame.

LICENSING AND CERTIFICATION

Nursing homes must be licensed by the state in which they operate. Although licensing requirements vary by state, most states require some combination or all of the following.

- On-staff physicians.
- On-staff registered nurses or licensed practical nurses available 24 hours per day.
- Demonstrations that the facility follows accepted medical practice in preventing injury to residents due to accidents or infection.
- Adequate bed space for the number of residents.
- Adequate bathing, toilet, and laundry facilities for the number of residents.
- Adequate food service facilities for the number of residents.

Most states determine whether a facility meets the requirements for licensing through on-site inspections. Depending on the state, these inspections may be performed at the time of the initial licensing or periodically during the time the facility is open. Some states conduct "surprise" visits every nine to twelve months to ensure that a facility is still in compliance with licensing requirements.

In addition to licensing by the state in which it operates, a nursing home must also obtain certification by the Federal government before it can receive Medicare or Medicaid payments. The requirements for Federal certification and state licensing are very similar. Most states not only perform on-site inspections for themselves but also for the Federal government.

Other than the state and Federal government, third-party private accreditation may also be obtained from the Joint Commission on the Accreditation of Health Care Organizations ("Joint Commission").

The Joint Commission establishes the standards that a nursing home must meet to receive accreditation. These standards include demonstrations (through on-site visits and written evaluations) that:

- the nursing home has adequate written medical records and procedure to document the care of residents;
- medications were stored safely and properly; and
- a plan of care was developed for each resident.

You should note that the only true *requirement* a nursing home must obtain is a state license. Nursing homes are subject to Federal standards only if they want to obtain Medicare or Medicaid payment. And accreditation by the Joint Commission is a voluntary process which the nursing home initiates itself.

So, what protection do these licenses, certifications, and accreditations really provide? Do they ensure that your elderly loved one will be safe? Well fed? Attended to when she cries out for help? No they will not. There is no assurance that abuse or neglect will not occur even if the nursing home you select is state-licensed and Federally certified and accredited by the Joint Commission. But screening nursing homes to ensure that they have these credentials will decrease the likelihood that abuse or neglect will occur. Here are some other steps you can take to help ensure a high level of care for your loved one.

- Surprise visits. Some nursing homes require that family members schedule visits in advance. Others allow or even encourage surprise visits. Nursing homes that encourage unscheduled visits should be strongly preferred over those that do not allow such visits. During your visit, note whether a resident's call for help is being attended to. It's important to take note of how *all* residents—not just your loved one—are being cared for. Neglect is often random and that elderly gentleman being ignored on the day you visit your mom could very easily be getting the treatment your mom will receive the day *after* your visit.
- Check the condition of the bathrooms and kitchen.
- Learn the names of all staff members, professional and nonprofessional, who have access to your loved one. Before your loved one moves into the nursing home, find out whether the home conducts background checks of its personnel, including checks for criminal records. It's important to check the staff or visiting physicians' backgrounds as thoroughly as possible since doctors whose licenses have been suspended in one state can and do receive licenses to practice in other states. Be alert to the histories of doctors who have moved from state to state and try to track down information on their license histories in previous states in which they have practiced. Also, be especially alert to service as a military physician. The military does not automatically disqualify doctors from enrolling as military physicians even if such doctors have had incidences of questionable conduct in the past. Though clearly many military physicians are the best in their professions—after all, some even care for the president of the United States—others benefit from a less than absolutely stringent military admissions system.
- Calling at a set time each day or week will give you a more accurate picture of the quality of service being provided.
- Get involved in any support groups of those with loved ones at the nursing home. This kind of involvement will give you access to more information about the overall quality of care at the nursing home. Such a group may also act as an advocate

for residents' care, a possibly stronger voice than yours alone. There's strength in numbers, as the saying goes.

- Contact your state's long-term care ombudsman (see list in appendix).
- Obtain the annual inspection report of the Health Care Financing Administration. Nursing homes that receive Medicare or Medicaid payments are inspected annually, and the results of that inspection are included in a report which the nursing home must provide to public requests.

12

Assisted Living
Residences

Joan and her husband Marty are both in their seventies. She was a homemaker. He retired from a corporation fifteen years ago. They've lived comfortably in their own home all these years and are basically in good health. Now, however, they could each use a little help in making sure that they've taken their medications. Joan is having trouble keeping up with the housekeeping and cooking. Recently they've begun to consider moving. But where should they go?

Assisted living programs can benefit people such as Joan and Marty, who need help with activities of daily living such as bathing, eating, dressing, or toileting. Most programs provide three meals a day, housekeeping, medication monitoring, and help with activities of daily living. If medical care is needed, it's usually provided by a facility that has a contract with the assisted care program.

These facilities are licensed by the state, usually under the auspices of the departments of health or social services. Although the terms vary from state to state, assisted living residences are also called domiciliary homes, group homes, rest homes, and retirement homes. So it's important not to assume that you will receive certain services. When seeking information, ask for specifics about what is provided.

In the interest of supporting the resident's independence and privacy, most programs offer private or semi-private rooms that are accessible only by key. In more modern facilities, bathrooms and kitchenettes are part of each apartment. Staff is available on a 24-hour basis.

State regulations typically prohibit staff in assisted living programs from providing medical care. Usually, registered nurses come to the facility to render care. These facilities are designed with the goal of maintaining the individual's right to have as much independence, privacy, and choice in life as possible. With that goal in mind, many facilities allow pets, use of alcoholic beverages, and maintain flexible visiting hours. Safety is a prime consideration, and apartments are often equipped with an emergency response system.

Daily rates range from $33 to $55 per day. Many services and amenities are often included in a monthly fee. For example, this may include menu selection of meals, scheduled transportation, housekeeping service, and programs to enrich the resident intellectually, spiritually, or socially. Residents can pay extra for amenities such as barber or beauty services, cable television, and other personal care services.

Medical consultations, pharmacy services, and services such as physical therapy can also be provided in the home and are billed to the resident by his or her health care provider.

Residents move from these residential programs to reside elsewhere when an increased level of medical care is consistently needed. When considering whether this is a good arrangement for your relative, determine whether it meets his current needs and what conditions would make him no longer eligible to reside there. For example, problems such as dementia, becoming bedridden or consistently incontinent, or displaying abusive behavior toward others, may be reasons for being asked to leave.

Some assisted living facilities have fewer than ten residents, whereas others have dozens of residents. Take into consideration the type of environment your relative would feel most comfortable living in.

13

Home Health Care Services

Home health care services are often appropriate for people who are recovering from hospitalization due to chronic illnesses such as diabetes or cardiopulmonary disease, for those who are terminally ill, or for those who have suffered a heart attack or stroke. Those who need help with activities of daily living (bathing, dressing, food preparation) can also benefit from this type of care.

Home health care is helpful to those who have been discharged from the hospital and need continued rehabilitative services, those who have chronic conditions that need to be monitored, and those who are unable to care for their personal needs without help.

There are many benefits to remaining at home despite physical limitations. By doing so, the person is able to remain in a familiar, comfortable setting. It can also be financially beneficial when compared with the cost of nursing home care or other types of living arrangements. Most importantly, remaining in the home helps a person feel independent.

Services that can be provided in the home include skilled nursing care, personal care, physical or speech therapy, and dialysis. Medical equipment and supplies can be rented or purchased for use in the home. Family and friends can assist with care in addition to the care provided by the health care agency.

Home health care can be provided by public or private hospitals, nonprofit or for-profit agencies, and public health departments. Medicare will cover the cost of skilled nursing or

87

rehabilitative services if they have been approved by a physician, and the person is unable to leave the home to receive the service.

Different levels of care can be provided in the home. When intensive services are needed, a physician or nurse comes to the home to give intravenous treatments or feedings, administer blood tests, or take x-rays. For those who need less intensive or intermediate services, a home health aide or licensed practical nurse comes to the home to administer medication or to help with bathing.

Rehabilitation services such as physical, occupational, or speech therapy can also be provided in the home. For those requiring this level of care, a nurse or physician may come periodically to the home.

Others may need even less intensive care. For these people, a health care aide comes to the home regularly to assist with activities of daily living such as bathing, dressing, and eating. Medical equipment such as insulin kits, oxygen, wheelchairs, and walkers can also be provided for home use.

In many communities, other types of in-home service are available such as barbers and dental and eye care services.

When you contact an agency about home health care services, the first person you speak with is often the intake worker who answers your questions and briefly assesses your needs on the telephone.

The intake worker will refer you to a social worker who will provide case management services. The social worker will help you find the services you need, help review your insurance coverage and financial needs, and help you find resources for funding. After meeting or talking with a social worker, you may be referred to a nursing coordinator, a professional trained in public health or geriatrics. The nursing coordinator will monitor the care your relative will receive.

As you can see, a number of different kinds of professionals may be involved in providing care to your loved one. The procedures and services that each can perform are dictated by state law and agency policy.

To ensure that you are getting the right care by the right person, you need to know which individual does what.

The following table summarizes the kinds of home health care providers and the type of licensing and certification required for them to operate.

Type of Provider	Type of Care	Licensing Required
• Home health care aide or attendant	• Bathing, dressing, watching, keeping company, reminding client to take medication, setting a glass of water on a bedside table; changing bed linens	• None required Training: up to 60 hours of training and completion of a supervised internship
• Registered Nurse (RN)	• Drawing blood; giving intravenous fluids through IV lines; giving injections	• 2-year certificate 3-year school of nursing or college degree in nursing plus a state licensing examination
• Licensed Nurse (LPN)	• Cannot draw blood; works under the supervision of a doctor or an RN. Administer oxygen, give enemas, check blood pressure, dress wounds, give medications (depending on the state)	• Completion of practical training program that typically lasts a year plus passing a state licensing examination
• Certified rehabilitative RN	• Same as RN but are specially trained in rehabilitation needed for patients who, for example, may have suffered strokes, heart attacks, or had hip replacements	• Same as RN certification in rehabilitation work
• Respiratory therapist	• Drawing blood to test oxygen levels, check equipment, monitor breathing	• Completion of a 2- or 4-year program culminating in a degree; some may also have obtained certification from The National Board for Respiratory Therapy

Type of Provider	Type of Care	Licensing Required
• Occupational therapist	• Help improve ability to perform tasks such such as bathing and eating	• Typically have received some formal training, may include certification
• Physical therapist	• Help improve limb mobility and ability to function through use of exercise, massage, prosthesis, or aids such as walkers • Can teach caregivers how to help with exercises	• Typically have received specialized training and are licensed by the state
• Speech therapist	• Improve ability to speak, recognize speech, enunciate; such abilities may have been damaged from birth or from causes such as stroke	• Many states require a license; most speech therapists have a master's degree; some may be certified by the American Speech and Hearing Association

HOME HEALTH CARE PROVIDERS—LICENSING AND CERTIFICATION

Licensing and certification requirements for home health care providers vary from state to state. They also vary depending on the type of care being provided.

As a general rule, the more basic or unskilled the care being provided, the greater the likelihood that no licensing at all is required.

Best Sources for Home Health Care

The best source for referrals of home health care agencies or workers is friends and family members who've had first-hand experience with the agency or worker and who can vouch for their competence, compassion, and honesty. Any names given to you by your most intimate and trusted network of friends and colleagues are likely to be just the kind of people with whom you would feel safe, entrusting the care of your elderly loved one.

Unfortunately, few of us are ever so lucky. Where else can we go to find the names of good workers?

National Organizations

Among national organizations, the following offer lists of home health care agencies.

- Foundation for Hospice and Home Care
  513 C St., NE
  Stanton Park
  Washington, DC 20002
  (202) 547-6586
- National Association for Home Care
  (Same address as Foundation for Hospice and Home Care)
- National Association of Professional Geriatric Care Managers
  1604 N. Country Club Rd.
  Tucson, AZ 85716
  (602) 881-8008
  (to provide names of geriatric managers in your area who in turn may give you names of good local home health care agencies and workers)
- National Home Caring Council
  (Same address as Foundation for Hospice and Home Care)
- National League for Nursing, Community
  Health Accreditation Program
  350 Hudson St.
  New York, NY 10014
  (212) 989-9393
- Visiting Nurse Association of America
  3801 E. Florida Ave., Suite 900
  Denver, CO 80210
  (303) 753-0218

Local Organizations

- Area agency on aging
- Churches
- Home health care agencies in the yellow pages of your telephone directory
- Health department

Who Does What and How They Can Help You

As the coordinator of the care plan, the social worker provides referrals to other needed services or agencies and works with everyone to maintain an effective care plan.

Input from family members can help figure out whether there are undetected problems in the way that care is being provided.

A nurse practitioner (NP) is a registered nurse who has successfully completed training in addition to the course of study noted above. In some states, a nurse practitioner can work without direct supervision by a physician. The Visiting Nurses Association sends nurses to the home to provide care. They also will teach the caregiver how to change dressings. And, they supervise the care provided by the home health aide.

A certified rehabilitative nurse (CRRN) is a registered nurse who has received additional training and earned certification in rehabilitative medicine. The CRRN formulates a plan for rehabilitation and then supervises the therapist.

Licensed vocational nurses (LVN) and licensed practical nurses (LPNs) have one year of training and have taken the state licensing exam. These health care providers are qualified to render routine care under supervision of a registered nurse or a physician. They perform tasks such as monitoring blood pressure, changing dressings, and administering oxygen.

Rehabilitation therapists can help your loved one regain the ability to function after a stroke or injury. For example, physical therapists help to improve limb mobility and function through use of exercise, massage, prostheses, or aids such as walkers. They can show caregivers how to help with the exercises. Physical therapists have received specialized training and are licensed by the state.

Occupational therapists design and implement a program to help improve your loved one's ability to perform tasks such as bathing, eating, and other everyday activities. They can also help family members learn how to help the person perform these activities.

Speech therapists and speech pathologists treat those who are unable to speak clearly due to injury, illness, or other chronic condition. Their goal is to help with recovery from speech and swallowing problems. When necessary, they recommend adaptive devices. They have earned a master's degree and, in many states, it is required that they have a license. Some have received professional certification from the American Speech and Hearing Association.

Respiratory therapists or inhalation therapists administer care and monitor patients with conditions related to breathing difficulty. They make certain that respiratory equipment is functioning properly and also teach the patient how to perform self-care routines. These therapists have graduated from a 2- or 4-year program. Some have also received certification from the National Board for Respiratory Therapy.

Home attendants (or home health aides) provide nonmedical patient care. They have received up to 60 hours of training and have completed a supervised internship. They are supervised by an agency. Their job duties include changing soiled linen, helping with bathing, dressing, and eating, supervising prescribed exercises, and preparing basic meals.

Homemakers help people who have stable, chronic conditions that interfere with their ability to function. They are supervised by an agency or by you if hired privately. Homemakers prepare meals, clean the laundry, and complete errands.

How Do You Choose an Agency?
As with most personnel services, the best way to find a good home health care agency is through referrals. There's no substitute for references from friends and family who've used a service. In addition to referrals, the following sources can also help you find an agency.

- Yellow pages of the telephone book.
- Churches.
- National organizations.

The Visiting Nurse Association of America is one of the oldest home health care providers in the country. Your church or synagogue, as well as community organizations, may have information about individuals or agencies whom they recommend to provide these services.

Call and ask if the agency provides the services you need. Ask about financial eligibility criteria. Request that written information be mailed to you. Check out whether the agency is licensed. Has the license ever been suspended? Is the license conditional? Why? Has there recently been an on-site inspection? Contact your Better Business Bureau to see if any complaints have been filed. How were they resolved?

Once you have decided to use a particular agency, an assessment of need must be done so that a "plan of care" or "care plan" can be made. A registered nurse does an in-person assessment, an interview, and an assessment of the home. A physical exam and a review of medical history is also done. Consultation with your health care provider should also occur. Recommendations should be discussed with you and your relative. Talk about any concerns either of you have and any problems that you foresee.

From this assessment, a care plan is formed that specifies what type of service is to be given, how often, who will provide the service (care), and what is the goal of the service.

The agency typically will send you a candidate to be interviewed for the position of your care provider. But you should make sure that you interview several candidates. Although the agency may charge you extra, it will be well worth it. After all, you want a care provider who is not only qualified and competent, but who also is compatible with your loved one and who is caring.

Make sure you know what services are not covered by your insurance. Check bills carefully. Keep your own records so that you can refer to them if necessary and so that you are certain of what you have been billed for.

How to Find Home Health Care Services

You can find home health agencies by using the following resources: your physician, your social worker or hospital discharge planner. Ask friends and family. Contact your Area Agency on Aging or the Visiting Nurses Association. Ask at your place of worship. Look in the Yellow Pages. Even the Employee Assistance Program at your job may have information or benefits available to you.

In some cases, home health care is fully covered by Medicare. In order for care to be fully covered, the person must be essentially incapable of leaving the home to receive the service. In addition, skilled nursing or rehabilitation services must be needed, and their physician must have given approval for each of the specific services received.

To determine eligibility, contact your local social services agency or Area Agency on Aging listed in the government section of your telephone book. The Elder Care Locator can also provide information (1-800-677-1116 from 9 A.M. to 5 P.M.) if you provide the zip code and a description of the problem.

If you are hiring a worker yourself, check their references carefully. Request proof of training and certification. Follow-up by calling the licensing department relevant to the field of work.

What Problems Should You Anticipate?

While we hope that these problems do not arise, sometimes things do go wrong despite the best plans. Many elderly people resist the idea of having someone come into their home to help them on a daily basis. Pat M., for example, is a fifty-five-year-old retired nurse from northern New Jersey who, with her husband, has to arrange for a care provider for her ninety-year-old father-in-law and eighty-eight-year-old mother-in-law. "Pop used to sabotage Mom's day care worker. We had to hire six people in the space of a year. We'd hire them and he'd somehow get them fired by harassing them. It got to the point where he'd destroy the care plans we had for him and our plans for Mom as well. We finally hired a big woman whom he was afraid of and he ultimately obeyed her."

Even those who are used to having a housekeeper may be uncomfortable with having a stranger provide personal care. Or they may be worried about the cost of care. Talk with your relative before making these changes. Involve them in the discussion of what they need and how it will affect their finances. As in most situations, when you have a greater sense of control, you are more likely to cooperate. Remind them that the home worker will give them the liberty to remain in their own home and that it frees you from doing errands and chores for them while you are visiting.

Your mother may miss the closeness you shared as a result of you doing things such as brushing her hair. Try to maintain this type of contact. Touch is important. It soothes and reassures. It reaffirms the emotional connection between the two of you and eases feelings of loneliness and depression.

An antagonistic relationship can develop between the worker and your loved one. Sometimes this happens because your relative is not used to telling someone in a tactful manner what to do and how to do it. In other cases, the person may object to the worker's ethnic origin, color, or religion. A lifetime spent having such a viewpoint cannot easily be changed. You and your family must decide how you are going to deal with this problem. You can help your parent to address and perhaps to change the way he or she interacts with the worker. Remember that the dignity of the worker is also important, and your relative is likely to receive better care from someone who is treated respectfully, rather than from someone who is treated rudely.

The best circumstance is that, you, your relative, and the worker develop a partnership in working together to help your relative. Everyone likes to receive acknowledgment when they have done a good job. Remember to notice the positives, while constructively changing the negatives. Instead of criticizing, tell the worker how you want certain things done the next time. Don't assume that it was purposely done wrong.

If the problem remains, you may have to contact the agency to request a different worker or to hire from another agency. You could also use what is called "respite care" during the interim when you do not yet have another worker.

You may be concerned about the possibility that your relative will be victimized in some way by the worker. Abuse by in-home workers can take the form of physical abuse. However, workers can be abusive in less noticeable ways. For example, a worker may not work the full number of hours for which he or she is being paid. A worker may be present in the home but spend his or her time watching television or reading rather than doing the tasks for which they are being paid. The home care worker could prey on your relative's sympathy, seeking loans of money or paid time off from work.

Like many elderly people, your relative may be afraid to report this, fearing retribution, further harm or abuse, or loneliness. He may misperceive the worker's role as being that of a new friend. While you do want a good relationship to exist between the worker and your relative, it is important to make sure that roles, responsibilities, and expectations are clear and fair.

There are ways to safeguard against abuse and mistreatment. Guard against theft and fraud by safeguarding your relative's valuables and important documents. Family members should take time to be present during the first few home visits and to periodically make unplanned, unannounced visits. If neighbors are willing to help, ask them to check on your relative from time to time when the worker is there. Talk to your relative and ask questions about how their day has been spent. Pay attention to any changes in behavior or appearance that could indicate a problem.

If you hire a health care worker on your own, without using an agency, be careful. Write a contract that specifies days off, vacation, your policy on lateness and absences, and notification necessary in case you or the worker decide to terminate employment. To protect yourself and your relative, have a secondary plan that includes people who can help you if the worker does not show up and you have to get to the office.

Make certain that the worker is fully aware of dietary restrictions, medication requirements, and a plan of what to do in an emergency. The worker may not be familiar with your relative's neighborhood, so inform them of directions to your house as well as of family or friends that they can call on if necessary.

14

Housing Options for Independent Living

Most of us want to live in our own house or apartment because the things around us are familiar and we are comfortable. Living in our own home also gives us privacy, helps us feel independent, and when it is mortgage-free, is economical. However, for the elderly, living alone can cause safety problems, loneliness, and social isolation. It is also hard for the elderly to maintain their house in good repair on their own.

For elderly who want to live *near* their family members without actually living in the same home, there is an option called "ECHO housing." The term "ECHO" stands for Elder Cottage Housing Opportunity. This type of housing is not available in every state and can only be built in areas with applicable zoning laws. ECHO houses typically are portable, prefabricated homes installed near the home of a relative. Although they differ in structure and design, most homes consist of a bathroom, kitchen, dining/living room area, and one or two bedrooms.

The benefit of an ECHO home is that privacy is maintained, and living costs are usually lower than they would be otherwise. However, the unit could affect the resale value of the relative's home and the tax valuation of the property.

Other elderly people choose to live in retirement apartments and communities. Retirement residences vary in size and structure and are often subsidized by Federal and state governments. Those built by private developers cost more, but there is often a shorter waiting list or no waiting list at all. These residences are built with the needs of the elderly in mind, so there are safety features such as easy-grip handles and doorknobs, as well as ramps or elevators.

RETIREMENT COMMUNITIES

The trend of "reverse migration" has boosted sales of retirement homes, because people have come to realize that they do not want to live so far away from their families. They decide to move closer to their families, yet continue to live on their own. Browse through the real estate section of your newspaper, and you may see advertisements for "active adult communities." These newly built residences for the older yet still active adult often feature services such as housekeeping, scheduled activities, meals, transportation services, and security.

These communities offer companionship and recreation. There is usually a range of amenities and services available to meet their needs, and this affects the maintenance fees.

These communities hold less appeal for those who prefer to live among people of various age groups.

CONGREGATE HOUSING

Congregate housing is another option. Residents live in one building and share all common living areas, yet have their own bedrooms and bathrooms. In most residences, at least one meal each day is eaten in the common dining room. Residents are provided with social and recreational activities. Services such as housekeeping and transportation are also available.

Congregate housing is most often used by people who are seventy-five years of age or older and who do not need 24-hour monitoring or assistance with activities of daily living. However, those that do not like to participate in group activities are not likely to prefer this option.

Through the Congregate Housing Services Program, the Federal government has funded congregate housing developments in 33 states.

Shared housing is another option. This exists when two or more unrelated people live in the same apartment or house and share living space, household expenses, and responsibilities. Zoning laws may prohibit this type of arrangement, but a variance may be granted if the homeowner is older than sixty years old.

HOME-SHARING

Home-sharing may be an option for those who do not want to live with relatives and who do not need medical help or rehabilitation, but do want company and the knowledge that they are not alone, especially at night.

This is different than hiring live-in help and it is important to know what you need and expect, before you let someone move in with you. Many people who agree to a home-sharing arrangement do so with the expectation that during the day they will be able to attend school or go to work. Others view it as employment and therefore expect to receive a salary.

Specify your expectations during the interview process. If you need the person to be home during the day, you must be able to pay them to compensate for their inability to gain employment elsewhere.

The more you can describe the tasks that are going to be part of the job, the better your chances are of avoiding potential conflict and finding the right person.

The personalities of each person have to be taken heavily into account when considering who will share your home. If the person likes to play music all day or at loud levels, you may not be compatible. For others, this may not be a problem. Generational differences also matter. If you don't want the person to have company or have a guest of the opposite sex spend the night, this has to be stated up front.

Many elderly people want someone to live with them so that they are not alone at night. Others primarily want companionship during the day. Others need someone to drive them on errands and to appointments. Still others choose this arrangement to help with expenses.

Many communities have agencies that match home seekers with those wanting to share their homes. You can also place ads in the newspaper. Verify information thoroughly. Use the same precautions that you would use when hiring anyone that will be entering and living in your home.

When helping your relative decide on any type of living arrangement, check to make sure that the home can safely accommodate an elderly resident.

Important safety factors to be considered include:

- Are there smoke detectors?
- Is there good lighting so that those with failing vision can see?
- Is it fall-proof?
- Is the bathroom equipped so that there are shower seats or railings?
- Are telephones accessible and located in more than one area?
- Are easy-to-read emergency telephone numbers placed near each phone?
- Are there many stairs or hard to reach rooms?

HOUSING OPTIONS AT A GLANCE

Shared Housing	Description	Cost
	Roomate Situation	Depends on Arrangement
Congregate housing	Group housing	200-50 location/services
Accessory homes/ ECHO homes	Small apartment built on the property of a single family home; single level designed to accommodate elderly needs	Cost of renovations about $125,000
Assisted living not covered by Medicare or provision	Ranges from large houses to multiapartment complexes; offers meals, transportation, and help with bathing	Ranges from $300 to $3000/month not covered by Medicare or most insurance plans
Continuing care community	Housing arrangement that offers varying levels of care and supervision; ranges from assisted living residences to nursing home	Entrance fee ($75,000 or more) plus rents from $500 to $3000/month
Nursing home	24-hour medical care provided	$30,000 to $100,000/year if covered by insurance; fees range depending on level of care provided
Apartments for senior citizens	Some are government subsidized	Long waiting list; available only to individuals with low income

15

Continuing Care Communities

Continuing care communities offer residents a combination of different types of housing and facilities. In this type of community, independent housing, assisted living residences, and skilled nursing facilities are all located within the same living complex or at least nearby. The defining characteristic of a continuing care community is the inclusion of a health care facility for residents.

You can qualify to live in this type of community if, upon entry, you are in reasonably good health, you're able to care for yourself, you can walk without assistance, and you are able to participate in group meals. You must also be financially able to afford the fees and expenses currently as well as in the future. Most residents have Medicare or other health care coverage.

Housing in these communities varies in size, layout, and type. They can be high-rise apartments with adjoining medical facilities or small living units with separate nursing facilities. The community may include townhouses, detached homes, efficiencies, or apartments.

Residents receive an all-inclusive package of services and amenities, in addition to readily available medical care. Meals are served in a central location. Social, cultural, religious, and recreational activities are provided.

The cost of living in this type of community is considerable; therefore the risk is substantial. Residents pay an entry fee also called a founder's fee or endowment. This can range from $20,000 to $400,000 depending on the type of health care coverage, the size of the living unit, the number of people covered, and the types of services included. Monthly fees of $500 to $3,000 are then charged. There is often a waiting period although many such communities are being built to meet the demand.

Since there is great risk and considerable cost involved, it's crucial that you think carefully about whether this is the best choice for your relative. Ask the following questions of the management when considering this move.

• What happens when you need to move into a nursing facility and all of the beds are occupied?
• Which services are included in the basic monthly fee?
• Which services is management planning to change or add?

Visit the site and plan to stay for a few days so that you have time to look at all the different living quarters, since you may someday live in each of them. Evaluate the independent living quarters, the assisted living residences, and the skilled nursing facility. Take notice of the way that the staff and the residents relate to one another. How are problems handled? What are the mealtimes like? How is the menu? Talk with new residents to see how they have adjusted. Talk with residents who have lived there for a few years to find out whether services have been maintained or whether quality is declining. Will your relative use most of the amenities that he will be paying for? If he wants to use the exercise room regularly, will that be possible or is it always full? How is time allotted so that each person gets to do those activities they are interested in doing?

There are different types of plans to choose from:

• *Extended (all-inclusive) contracts.* All services needed, including unlimited nursing care, are covered by the entry fee and the monthly fee.
• *Modified contracts.* The resident is allowed only a certain number of days of nursing care per year. If he needs more care he is charged at a rate (usually 80 percent of the full rate).
• *Fee-for-service contracts.* Residents are provided with independent living and assisted living services. If they need any nursing care, they must pay 100 percent of the cost for that care.

16

Medical Equipment and Adaptations to the Home

You've decided that you want to care for your relative in your home. Or, you've decided to hire in-home care so that your relative can stay in his or her home. The next task is to safety-proof the home and buy or rent the necessary adaptive devices based on recommendations from the therapists and physicians involved in providing care for your relative.

Your goal should be to provide an environment that is safe yet challenging and that allows for as much independence as possible.

Accident prevention is the first priority. Elderly people often have difficulty climbing stairs, getting in and out of the bathtub or shower, and turning door knobs and handles. Falling and slipping will occur unless adequate precautions are taken.

Bars and rails in the bathtub and near the toilet help them maneuver safely. Ramps help them get in or out of the home and from one level in the home to another. Handrails in hallways provide support, and grab bars and transfer benches aid mobility. Nonskid mats should be placed in the shower. Throw rugs should not be used anywhere in the home because they can cause your relative to slip and fall.

Night-lights help the elderly see if they have to get out of bed during the night and can prevent initial confusion if they awaken in the dark. Since the elderly are prone to burns from extreme temperatures, keep the hot water heater at no more than 110° F.

All emergency phone numbers should be written clearly and placed next to telephones, along with your relative's address and basic directions to their home. Sometimes people panic in times of emergency or they may be too ill or disoriented to remember these facts when talking to emergency services.

Problems with heating or ventilation are common. The Weatherization Assistance Program (WAP) of the United States Department of Energy will pay for the homes of low income citizens to be weatherized.

Funding for home modification and repair can be found in many sources and is designated for those elderly who are eligible to receive it. Many communities use community development block grants to help residents maintain or modify their homes. Your local Area on Aging can give you information about funds from the Older Americans Act Title III that can be used for these purposes.

The provisions of the Fair Housing Act of 1988 now require new construction of dwellings with four or more units to include wheelchair accessibility, reinforced walls so that grab bars and rails can be installed, and accessible thermostats and electrical outlets.

Help your relative make plans to have work done on their house. The elderly often fall prey to con artists who claim they will make repairs but only get paid in advance, and then disappear. Take charge of the hiring process. Hire a licensed and bonded contractor. Get bids from a few contractors. Ask for references from past customers and call to speak with them. Check with the Better Business Bureau.

Although modifications to the home may not be needed, medical equipment may be. Devices such as the hoyer lift can help your relative move in and out of bed, as well as to get up from a seated position. Bath benches are waterproof chairs that go in the bathtub so that one can slide from the rim of the tub into the tub. A raised toilet seat is another useful device. Medicare pays for the rental or purchase of home care equipment if a physician certifies that it is medically necessary. Nonprofit home health care agencies, senior citizen centers, and organizations such as the America Society and Multiple Sclerosis Society often sell reconditioned equipment. Keep safety in mind when looking to save money. It is important that all equipment be in good condition and properly cleaned.

17

Use of Community Services

NUTRITION PROGRAMS

For those who cannot prepare their own meals, a service such as Meals On Wheels, which delivers hot, nutritionally balanced meals to the home can be helpful. The national hotline for Meals on Wheels is (800) 999-6262.

Programs such as Meals On Wheels are helpful to those who cannot easily get to the grocery store and to those who are unable to cook for themselves because of physical disability or mental incapacity. Participation in these programs can improve their intake of nutritious meals, which is necessary to stay healthy or to recover from illness. Most programs deliver meals five days per week, and, in some areas, also on weekends. In addition to hot meals, a cold meal that is prepared for heating is also delivered. In some areas, special menus are available for those who have dietary restrictions because of religious beliefs. In some communities, church or neighborhood groups organize meal delivery programs.

In addition to improving nutrition, this type of program also provides regular social contact for the homebound person. And, in the event that the resident does not answer the door when the meal is delivered, the delivery person may be able to let you know if your relative is sick and needs help.

Problems do sometimes occur. Some elderly people suffer from memory loss and may forget to eat the meals or to prepare them properly by reheating them thoroughly. Some people do not have ovens to heat the meals. Others may not like the taste of the food. In that instance, family members can spice up the meals according to dietary restrictions. These types of problems need to be monitored by a family member or friend. Meal delivery programs are usually licensed by the local health department.

TRANSPORTATION SERVICES

Transportation services may be available for those who need help getting to and from places such as their doctor's office or the grocery store.

Grocery stores, doctor's offices, beauty salons, and banks are not always within easy walking distance. Those who cannot drive are therefore cut off from access to these services. Family and friends can be a big help. However, relying on others to drive you from place to place can sometimes be time-consuming and frustrating. Most people don't like to feel dependent on family to take them places. Without access to social activities, one can easily become socially isolated.

Many elderly drivers are reluctant to admit when they are having difficulty driving. However, arthritis, back and joint stiffness, slowed reaction time, vision problems, memory loss, and hearing problems often contribute to difficulty driving. Giving up one's driving privileges is often another loss faced by the elderly. Like one's home, one's car is for many people an important part of their identity and proof of their independence and well-being. Classes are given by the motor vehicle department to retrain the elderly. Often, driving rules have changed since they took their first test to get a license. In addition, they have to learn to compensate for their decreased agility and response time. Many elderly drivers limit the areas in which they drive. For example, they no longer get on the highway to go to the shopping mall. Instead, they go to local stores that are closer and require less driving time.

Mechanical adaptations such as hand controls, extra warning signals, glare-reducing glass, and adapted brake and gas pedals can be helpful. To find out where these devices can be obtained, contact your motor vehicle department or the occupational therapy department at a local hospital.

Transportation services include reduced fare eligibility on public transportation systems, special van service to appointments or errands, and taxi service. Advance reservations are usually required for special van service. To locate transportation services in your relative's community, contact your local Area on Aging or call the Eldercare Locator (1-800-677-1116). The National Transit Hotline also provides information about transit services for the elderly and disabled (1-800-527-8279). You can also look in the Yellow Pages or refer to your state government listings for the state office on aging or the human resources department. Some services offer door-to-door service. Advance reservation is usually required, and a fee may be charged.

Some transportation services take the elderly to senior centers, medical appointments, and social activities. These services can relieve family members of including this task in their daily activities.

Ride-sharing programs in which volunteers drive people where they want to go are also offered in some areas.

Services such as in-home dental care, barber services and vision care services are also provided in some communities. Chore services are often available to provide help with heavy and seasonal cleaning and household repairs. Programs subsidized by the government are available in some states. Commercial firms, whom you pay privately, are available in each state. They can provide services such as visiting nurse services, homemaking services, and telephone checking programs.

Telephone reassurance services staffed by senior citizen volunteers call on a regular basis to ensure the well-being of the homebound resident. Community volunteers usually call at a specified time and are trained to listen closely to determine if there is a problem. If no one answers their phone call, the volunteer notifies the program supervisor who then contacts a family member or implements other prearranged plans to check on the resident. Many utility companies have elder-watch programs. In many areas, gas and electric companies train their employees to keep an eye out for those elderly residents who live alone and notify the authorities when they suspect a problem.

Emergency response systems may be useful for those who are functioning well on their own but fear that in an emergency no one would know they need help. These systems come in many different forms. One system works so that your elderly relative wears a necklace or bracelet that has a button they can push if needed. When the button is pushed, a signal is received by a unit next to a receiver near the phone. It in turn dials a response center. Your relative is identified by a code at the response center. Someone in the response center will then call your relative. If they do not get an answer, an emergency team is sent to the home. This type of alert system can usually be purchased or rented. They range in price from $200 to $2,000 plus a monthly service fee. Rental fees range from $20 to $50 monthly after paying an installation fee.

Shop around to see which system best suits your needs. Find out whether the response team is near your relative's home. Get specific information about the training of the staff and the response center's average response time. Make sure that your relative can speak clearly to be understood and is able to hear and understand others on the phone. Inquire as to whether you can try a system for a trial period and if you can receive a money-back guarantee. Remember that the system has to be kept in working condition in order for it to be of use; if batteries are required, check them regularly to make sure they work. When you visit your relative, make sure that all wires or cords are still properly connected and working.

Another volunteer program that benefits the homebound is the friendly visitors program in which people come to the home to visit. During the visit, they can sit and talk, help the resident write letters, listen to music together, read to them, and join them in any pleasurable activity.

In some communities, grocery shopping can be done by telephone or computer. You can determine if these services are available in your area by contacting your local senior citizens center, checking your library or phone book, or asking your hospital discharge planner.

18

Hospice Care

Your loved one has been diagnosed as having a terminal illness. She wants to be discharged from the hospital, and her physician has consented to this because she can receive the care she needs at home.

Hospice care traditionally is based on the philosophy that death is a natural and inevitable part of life so that instead of trying to prolong a dying person's illness, the focus should be on providing them with an environment that enhances their remaining days.

Care is provided by a multidisciplinary team of health care professionals and trained volunteers. In some communities, hospices are independently located, whereas in other communities it is provided in the home or in the hospital.

The emotional and psychological needs of the patient are addressed, while medical care is simultaneously provided. The patient is provided with symptom control which can include the relief of problems such as pain, nausea, dizziness, constipation, depression, or severe insomnia.

Hospice care extends to the family of the ill person, not solely to the person. In this context, the process of caring for a terminally ill family is supported by a trained, caring staff. Issues of loss, separation, grief, and dying are worked through during the hospice stay. After the patient's death, hospice workers continue to work with the family during the bereavement process.

The hospice care team consists of physicians, a clinical nurse practitioner, nursing assistants or aides, socials workers, dietitians, pharmacists, physical therapists, chaplains, and trained volunteers. Some hospice programs use psychiatric services.

113

Admittance to hospice is usually granted only to those whose life expectancy is six months or less. This is important because it has a direct effect on payment eligibility. Most hospice services are covered by Medicare, provided that the hospice is certified and that the patient has been certified as terminally ill by the patient's doctor and the medical director of the hospice.

On admittance, the patient is examined by the hospice physician. A clinical nurse practitioner meets with the family to set up a care plan. The goals of the hospice program are reviewed, and participants are encouraged to express any concerns or problems they anticipate regarding their family member's care.

Palliative care is provided with the goal of easing the patient's journey toward death, by affirming his need for comfort and support in life. Treatments such as chemotherapy, ventilators, or feeding tubes are usually not implemented unless such treatment reduces pain.

The patient's medical needs are assessed through daily visits from the physician and the clinical nurse practitioner. The social worker helps the patient and his or her family to cope with the problems they face. Relationships are explored with an opportunity for reconciliation, closure, and expression of feelings.

Each person on the care team has a specific function. For example, the dietitian provides foods and snacks that enhance the appetite, since those who are ill often have no appetite, despite the importance of maintaining caloric input. Pharmacists provide the various medicines prescribed to alleviate pain or other symptoms. Physical therapists work with the patient to relieve discomfort, rather than to provide rehabilitation or to increase functioning.

Chaplains offer spiritual comfort and guidance in accordance with the family's religious or spiritual beliefs.

Volunteers have a very important role in hospice care because they are trained to provide much of the care that, if rendered by a therapist or an aide, would significantly raise the overall cost of care. Volunteers change bed linens, help with bathing and grooming, and provide the patient with company and support. In many hospice programs, volunteers are provided with training in grief and bereavement, disease processes, nursing procedures, and hospice philosophy.

Many hospice organizations provide home-care services and respite care for family caregivers. Hospice staff are usually available 24 hours a day and in case of emergency. In some communities, hospices maintain contracts with hospitals so that if more intensive medical care is needed as the patient reaches the end stages of life, transfer to the hospital can be easily arranged.

HOSPICE CARE IN THE HOME

Some families arrange for hospice care in their home. They want their relative to die in a familiar, comfortable environment. It is important to set up your home program so that you as the caregiver do not quickly burn out. Contact a home care agency to tell them what you are doing so that they can provide services such as visiting nurse and home health aide, to your home. Contact your social workers and pastor or clergyman and ask for their assistance. In-home hospice services can include respite care so that the caregiver can get rest, do household errands, or attend a wedding. Hospice workers can also teach the family how to provide care such as giving injections, learning how to help the person in and out of bed, and bathing and grooming.

HOSPICE CARE IN OTHER SETTINGS

When hospice care is provided in a hospital setting, family members and friends are encouraged to help care for their loved one. They eat meals with the patient, bathe and groom him, and provide various other types of care which would otherwise be done by a member of the hospital staff. Hospice care is similarly provided in nursing homes.

Hospice care is considered less costly than hospital care. Many insurance carriers, including Medicare and Medicaid, will reimburse payment for it.

To find out about hospice care in your community, contact The Hospice Association of America (202) 546-4759 to start your inquiry. Ask about certification, staffing, and eligibility for admission. You may contact HOSPICE LINK by phone at 1-800-331-1620, or write them at: Five Essex Square, P.O. Box 713, Essex, CT 06426.

19

Adult Day Care

Adult day-care centers are often thought to be the same as senior citizen centers; they are very different. Adult day-care centers provide health services and social services. They are designed to meet the needs of those with physical disability or memory loss. Rehabilitation therapy, medication, and basic nursing care are provided. Staff also assist with eating, grooming, and other personal care needs.

Transportation to and from the center is usually provided, as is at least one meal each day. One can attend one or more days per week on a prescheduled basis.

Adult day care is helpful for senior citizens who live alone and for those who live with family members who are away at work each day. The centers also provide respite for caregivers. Most importantly, however, it gives the elderly person a chance to meet with others their age, to enjoy activities, and to receive needed care.

The Veteran's Administration provides adult day care to eligible veterans. Others can locate centers by contacting your local Agency on Aging, looking in the Yellow Pages or the "Silver Pages," or asking at senior citizen centers.

In order to determine whether your relative would be comfortable in the center, visit and look around. Look at the menu. Read the activities list and check to make sure that the activities actually happen each day or week. Examine the rehabilitation equipment to be sure that it is in good condition. Ask if there is at least one person on the premises at all times who is trained in CPR. Ask about the center's emergency procedures. Stay there for awhile to give yourself and your relative a chance to see if they feel comfortable there. Are there others similar to them there? Do they seem congenial? How does staff interact with the participants?

The National Institute on Adult Day Care has compiled a list of standards to ensure quality day-care services. Centers are encouraged to meet these standards. The ratio of staff to adults should be one staff person for every eight adults. Before services are rendered to your relative, an assessment of his or her needs should be done, along with a plan that specifies how this will be done. For example, if rehabilitation therapy is recommended, the plan should state how often the therapy will be given, for how long, what types of therapy will be done, what the goal of the therapy is, and who will be the therapist.

Participants in the center should be given at least two weeks notice if the center wants to discharge them or terminate them. A written agreement about emergency care should be formulated. The center should provide a range of activities, including social activities, attention to physical care, and individual and group activities. The center should also be willing to coordinate its services with services offered by other programs.

For those who qualify, Medicaid will pay for adult day care. The cost can range from $20 to $150 per day, depending on the types of services provided and the region in which the center is located. Some centers have a sliding fee scale based on ability to pay.

It's important to make sure your relative is examined by a board-certified geriatrician or physician who has expertise in caring for the elderly. A nurse and social worker are also usually part of the geriatric care team. A thorough examination will assess physical health, mental state, and level of functioning. You can help the process by making certain that the physician is aware of the following information.

- Your parent's health history (past illnesses, injuries, hospitalizations, conditions).
- Past and current use of over-the-counter and prescription medications.
- Allergies and drug sensitivities.
- Problems with walking (e.g., tendency to trip or fall), problems with vision, memory loss.
- Aids used in functioning (e.g., eyeglasses, dentures, canes).

- Symptoms such as dizziness, nausea, fatigue, and swelling.
- Past and current emotional state—do they seem depressed, agitated, anxious? Do they talk about dying despite being healthy? Do they or any family members have a history of depression or other psychological problems?
- Difficulties with functioning (e.g., persistent inability to sleep, loss of appetite, weight gain, incontinence).
- Use of drugs or alcohol.
- Are they socially isolated?

PART FOUR
How to Pay for It

20

Will Medicare Take Care of It All?

For most of us, the answer to the question posed in the heading above is "no." However, let's look at what Medicare does and does not cover.

Medicare is a Federally established and Federally run insurance program. Medicare is available to you so long as you have a Social Security number, are a U.S. citizen, and are sixty-five years and older.

Medicare is a general insurance plan that provides hospital care to you for ninety days. It also covers nonhospital doctor-prescribed care under certain limited circumstances.

Let's say you are sixty-five and you sustain a hip fracture. Medicare will cover you for up to ninety days, with just a few provisions. First, starting with day sixty-one, you have to start paying $184 per day. That's your deductible under Medicare. And, even if you're there for less than sixty days, you still have to pay a deductible of $736. These figures are compiled based on 1996 standard so these totals may have changed.

If, for whatever reason, you're confined to the hospital for longer than ninety days, you're on your own. Medicare will not cover any hospital costs after ninety days. There's one caveat here that may save you a bit of money. Each of us is given a "lifetime reserve" of sixty days to be used to extend the ninety-day coverage if necessary. During this bonus period, your share of the costs

123

is $368 per day. Once the sixty days are used up, you can never receive additional Medicare coverage days.

Psychiatric hospital stays are treated differently. Medicare will cover up to 190 days in a psychiatric hospital.

As you can see, there are several important medical crises that Medicare doesn't cover. In addition, Medicare does not cover the following:

- A private duty hospital nurse;
- The first three pints of blood you receive in a hospital;
- A private room in a hospital unless it's deemed medically necessary;
- Nursing home care that is considered merely "custodial" as opposed to "skilled";
- Stays in a skilled nursing facility unless your stay follows a hospital stay of at least three days. Medicare will cover up to twenty days without requiring a co-payment from you. After twenty days, you will be required to pay a co-payment of $92 per day. Medicare will not cover any costs after one hundred days in a nursing home.
- Nursing care at home (only care provided through certified home care agencies and only if it is part-time or intermittent);
- Physician fees that are higher than the Medicare fee schedule;
- 20 percent of even approved, eligible physician charges;
- Prescription drugs which are not used while you are in the hospital. There's one exception here: Medicare will cover prescriptions for immunosuppressive (anti-rejection) drugs you use during the first year following an organ transplant;
- Dental treatments;
- Treatments for vision or hearing problems;
- Routine medical examinations with two exceptions. Medicare will cover mammogram screenings every two years and pap smears every three years;
- Routine foot problems;
- Medical care outside the United States, except for certain areas along the border;
- Chiropractic care that does not involve manipulation of the spine; and
- Respite (convalescent) care.

MEDICARE IS NOT MEDICAID

People often confuse Medicare with Medicaid. Medicare is an insurance policy for Americans over sixty-five. Medicaid is a health insurance program for poor Americans. Medicaid is a Federally funded program that is administered at the state level. State administration of Medicaid has produced a patchwork of inconsistencies, and it is possible that payments and service coverage will vary from state to state. A complete listing of Medicaid offices in each of the fifty states is included in the Appendix.

To qualify for Medicaid, you must be practically destitute. That's the bad news. The good news is that if you qualify for Medicaid it is far more comprehensive than Medicare. All your expenses are covered, far more services are provided than under Medicare, and you have no deductible or co-payment.

Some caregivers, overwhelmed with the staggering costs of providing care to suddenly ill parents, have adopted the drastic strategy of dumping their parents assets, impoverishing them just enough to qualify for Medicaid.

Should you adopt this strategy? You might choose this strategy if after reading about all the other options in this book you discover that you still will not have enough to make ends meet and provide a reasonably decent level of care for your parent.

MEDIGAP INSURANCE

Because Medicare is a medical safety net with gaping holes in it, neither you nor your parents can afford to rely solely on Medicare for your health care needs.

In response to the need to plug the obvious holes in Medicare coverage, private insurance companies over the years have developed insurance policies called "Medigap" policies.

As their name implies, Medigap policies attempt to fill in the gaps in medical coverage that exist under Medicare. Congress has imposed rules on private industry to simplify the types of policies being offered as Medigap. The hope was that simplification would eliminate potential abuses in sales practices in a market principally targeted at elderly consumers.

Federal law now requires Medigap insurance providers to classify the bundle of coverage benefits they offer into one of nine categories labeled "A" through "J." Category A Medigap policies offer the fewest benefits—and thus plug the fewest holes—while policy J is the so-called Cadillac plan, offering the widest range of benefits.

The chart on the following page displays the differences among the Medigap policies.

MEDIGAP PLANS COMPARISON GUIDE—STANDARD MEDICARE SUPPLEMENT PLANS

	Plan A	Plan B	Plan C	Plan D	Plan E	Plan F	Plan G	Plan H	Plan I	Plan J	Your Current Plan
Basic Benefits	✓	✓	✓	✓	✓	✓	✓	✓	✓	✓	Days 21–100 / Beyond 100 Days
Skilled Nursing Coinsurance	✗	✗	✓	✓	✓	✓	✓	✓	✓	✓	
Part A Deductible	✗	✓	✓	✓	✓	✓	✗	✓	✓	✓	
Part B Deductible	✗	✗	✓	✗	✗	✓	✗	✗	✗	✓	
Part B Excess	✗	✗	✗	✗	✗	✓ 100%	✓ 80%	✗	✓ 100%	✓ 100%	
Foreign Travel Emergency	✗	✗	✓	✓	✓	✓	✓	✓	✓	✓	
At Home Recovery	✗	✗	✗	✓	✗	✗	✓	✗	✓	✓	
Drugs	✗	✗	✗	✗	✗	✗	✗	✓ Basic $1250 Limit	✓ Basic $1250 Limit	✓ Extended $3000 Limit	
Preventative Care	✗	✗	✗	✗	✓	✗	✗	✗	✗	✓	

Use the space provided below for your product and cost worksheet

	PLAN A	PLAN B	PLAN C	PLAN D	PLAN E	PLAN F	PLAN G	PLAN H	PLAN I	PLAN J	YOUR CURRENT PLAN

✓ Included in Plan.
✗ Not Included in Plan.

Basic Benefits: The following are included in all plans:

> **Hospitalization:** Part A coinsurance (days 61–150) plus coverage for 365 days after Medicare ends
> **Medical Expenses:** The 20% Part B coinsurance
> **Blood:** The first three pints of blood

Note: Your current plan may offer benefits not available in the above plans; for example;

- Private room and private duty nursing
- Extended SNF care beyond Medicare's 100 days
- Prescription benefits with no caps
- Various ways to pay excess charges above Medicare approved charges

Reprinted with permission of the AARP.

Laws That Protect You*

The law increases safeguards for consumer protection. The following are medigap protections provided by federal law:

- You must receive an outline of coverage describing the benefits of your policy.
- You have 30 days to cancel a policy for a full refund of all premiums paid.
- It is illegal for an insurance company to claim affiliation with the government, Medicare, Social Security, etc.

*Copyright 1995, 1997, American Association of Retired Persons. All rights reserved.

- Medigap plans must return an average of at least 65 percent of premiums or $.65 per dollar (75 percent for group policies) to beneficiaries in claims. This is called the loss ratio. Some companies do not pay back enough even though the law requires it.
- Check with your state insurance department to make sure any plan you consider meets this target.
- The replacing insurer must waive any time periods that apply to pre-existing conditions and waiting periods for similar benefits to the extent such periods were met under the original policy.
- All policies since November 1990 must be guaranteed renewable. This means that companies cannot cancel or not renew a policy for any reason other than misrepresentation or nonpayment of premiums.
- Buyers cannot be denied a policy based on pre-existing conditions for the first six months of enrollment in Medicare, although the insurers can reserve the right to refuse coverage for particular claims due to pre-existing conditions for the first six months the policy is in effect.
- Companies are prohibited from selling duplicative policies. Applications for coverage must include questions to determine if the applicant already has medigap coverage or qualifies for Medicaid.
- Policies issued which are not Medicare supplement policies, but which the NAIC has determined might be mistaken for a Medicare supplement plan, must clearly state that, "This policy is not a Medicare Supplement Policy or that this is not Medicare Supplemental Insurance."
- Insurance companies that violate the law will face monetary penalties up to $25,000.
- States that already had standard medigap plans prior to the enactment of the new law may be granted an exemption and allowed to continue under their existing system. Massachusetts, Wisconsin, and Minnesota have existing standard plans.
- If you qualify for Medicaid, you cannot be sold a medigap policy unless Medicaid will pay your premium. Further, if you lose entitlement to Medicaid, you can resume under your old medigap policy without filing a new application.
- In 1997 doctors who do not accept assignment are not allowed to charge more the 15 percent above the Medicare fee schedule.

LONG-TERM CARE POLICIES

Louise wants to take care of Alice in her home for as long as she can. But, to her horror, she's discovered that Medicare simply doesn't cover the kind of care that Alice needs. Alice needs a lot of social interaction, she needs bathing on some days when she can't be coaxed to do it herself, and she needs to be fed. She also needs the mental stimulation from other seniors that she gets at the adult day-care center which Louise drives her to daily. She doesn't need what you might call "needle care," care that might involve giving injections or that provides other so-called "skilled nursing care." Medicare doesn't cover any of the care that Louise provides—called "custodial care"—and most of the Medigap policies won't cover all of it either.

An industry has been developed to plug this hole with "long-term care" policies. As their name suggests, long-term care policies will cover the cost of in-home or nursing home care over the life of the recipient. Nursing home care can cost from $30,000 to $80,000 annually. Who has that kind of money?

The price of long-term care policies increases with the age of the recipient. Therefore, it is important to start evaluating these policies *before you need them for your parent*. Let's look at a policy you might find in the market today.

AARP offers a group plan for its members through the Prudential Insurance Company. It offers the following benefits:

- Coverage for one or more necessary diagnostic, preventive, therapeutic, rehabilitative, maintenance, or personal care in a setting other than an acute care unit of a hospital, such as in a nursing home, in the community, or in the home.
- $50–75 per day, depending on the type of plan you choose, for stays in a nursing home 91 days or longer, up to a maximum of 1460 days (4 years).
- Covered home health care and adult day-care visits during a "benefit period" for visits greater than 46 (no benefits for the first 45 visits), up to seven visits per week and up to a lifetime maximum of 730 paid visits. The breakdown for particular types of home care is as follows:

Home nurse visit	$35 or $50
Home therapist visit	$35 or $50

| Home health aide visit | $25 or $35 |
| Adult day-care visit | $30 or $40 |

A benefit period begins when you receive care in a nursing home or receive a covered home health care or adult day-care visit and ends when you have not been confined in an eligible nursing home or received a covered home health care or adult day care visit for six consecutive months.

These benefits are fairly substantial. The monthly premiums depend on the age of the insured at the time that you buy the plan.

How do you comparison shop for long-term care policies? The following list provides important features to compare:

- Does the plan provide home health care and adult day-care benefits, and if so for how many visits? What is the lifetime maximum number of visits?
- How much does the plan pay for each home health care visit or adult day-care visit? Is there a weekly maximum number of visits?
- Does the plan restrict the benefits it will pay for home health care to health care providers, such as registered nurses, licensed practical nurses, qualified therapists, or qualified home health aides. If so, do you have a preferred provider who would be excluded by the restriction?
- Do the benefits increase to keep up with inflation?
- Do the premiums increase with passing time or inflation? If the premiums do increase, how long is the period of time during which premiums are guaranteed to be held flat?
- Does the plan have a "waiver of premium" provision which waives the requirement to pay premiums during certain events such as your disability or unemployment?
- Does the plan cover nursing home care? If so, how many days are covered and how much does the policy pay per day? Is there a lifetime maximum number of days covered?
- Are nursing home benefits paid for skilled, intermediate, and custodial nursing care?

Most major insurance companies offer some type of long-term care policy. It's a booming business. Using the questions above as your guide, you should call the major companies (their toll-free numbers are listed in the Appendix) and order long-term policy disclosures from at least six of them for comparison. Again, the younger the age of your elderly loved one, the lower the premium, so it pays to start shopping around now.

21

Reverse Mortgages and Other Ways to Use Your Home

Reverse mortgages are home equity loans that do not have to be repaid until the home is sold or the homeowner dies. These products are called "reverse" mortgages because, unlike traditional mortgage loans where the cash flows out of your pocket into the bank, in a reverse mortgage the cash flows from the bank and into your pocket.

Reverse mortgages were created by lenders in the 1970s to address the needs of bank customers who were low on cash but who had big amounts of equity in their houses. The target customer is a middle income senior empty nester who has lived in her house for a long time and paid off the mortgage. Now, she's retired, so her monthly income is relatively low, and she needs cash to pay her bills. Other than her home, she has few assets.

Her home is a valuable asset, however. Purchased 30 years ago in a middle-class income for $25,000, it has now appreciated to a current market value of $300,000.

This is how a reverse mortgage works. The elderly relative would place a mortgage on her home in favor of the bank. The mortgage would provide for the tranference of the property upon the senior's death or at the time of the sale of the property—whichever comes first.

In exchange, the bank agrees to lend the senior a percentage of the home's market value. The percentage varies from bank to bank. Some banks lend up to 80 percent of the value, others cap the amount at 75 percent, and still others will lend up to 90 percent of market value. Check with banks in your area as well as with at least three national lenders (see Appendix D for a list of national lenders with reverse mortgage programs) to get the best deal you can.

In our example, the senior with the house valued at $300,000 might receive a lump sum of 80 percent ($240,000) of the value of her home. Some banks give customers the option of receiving the payment in installments designed to "pay down" the reverse mortgage over a fixed period of, say, 30 years. Again, check with at least three banks to compare pay off and payout options.

FEDERAL PROGRAMS

The Federal government insures certain reverse mortgages under a program administered by the Federal Housing Administration (FHA). Lenders participating in this program are insured against losses from customers who fail to repay the reverse mortgage.

REVERSE ANNUITY MORTGAGE

A reverse annuity mortgage is similar to the reverse mortgage discussed earlier. Taking the example again of our senior with the $300,000 house, if she obtained a reverse annuity mortgage, a bank typically would use the $240,000 lump sum to buy an annuity designed to pay her a monthly income for the rest of her life, based on an estimate of life expectancy such as the types used by insurance companies.

OTHER WAYS TO USE THE HOME TO RAISE CASH

Renting Out
Your house-rich, cash-poor relative can consider renting out a room (or more than one room). This practice has been around for

centuries in this country and internationally. The practice typically flourishes during hard times, such as during the Great Depression in the 1930s.

Operating a Home Business

The level of functioning of your elderly loved one may still be good enough to enable them to operate a home-based business. An elderly loved one who has difficulty walking but has a clear mind can operate a home tailoring business. Likewise, she may be able to write a newsletter in a field of interest. She may be able to bake specialty goods for resale to a local gourmet shop or school. She may be a home tutor offering remedial or enrichment lessons to help local students.

PART FIVE

Legal Documents

22

Wills, Power of Attorney, Advance Directives

Advance directives are different from living wills. Living wills are documents that basically either say "If I'm flat on my back and it looks like I'm going to die, you should pull the plug," or they may say, "If I'm flat on my back and things look bleak, hang in there, and never, ever, ever, pull the plug." Living wills, therefore, anticipate your immediate death.

Advance directives are instructions given to the medical doctors so that they know whom they should listen to or what should be done if the loved one is unconscious and unable to express his or her wishes. Like living wills, advance directives are letters that determine how you want to spend your future. However, the message in living wills and advance directives are quite different.

WHO'S IN CHARGE

Advance directives can take any number of forms. After all, they are letters you send to your future. The message in the letters is almost entirely up to you.

One message or instruction you can give is simply to designate the person you want the doctors to listen to and whose instructions you want the doctor to follow. These kind of advance directives act to designate your agent—your medical proxy.

Medical proxies or agents can be very powerful. You can literally give them the power of life and death depending on the language you choose. "I appoint Jane Doe as my medical proxy, having all powers as I would have were I conscious, to make all decisions affecting my health, including decisions having the risk of death."

Jane Doe, with this form in hand, would become your voice if you are unconscious and in need of medical care. Only a person in whom you have unshakable trust and who can make clear-headed reasoned decisions should ever be entrusted with this power.

Many adult children try to have their parents prepare advance directives. Unfortunately, many parents resist for the same reasons most of us don't ever get around to making wills: The thought of our own mortality scares us.

Assuming that we can convince our parents or loved ones to make an advance directive, and the form of the directive merely appoints a person to act without telling that person what decisions he or she should make, exactly what guidance should that person follow? How should they be guided in their decisions?

In the court cases that have involved advance directives, at least three standards have emerged to dominate the thinking about what kind of guidance is proper for Jane Doe to follow. As medical proxy for you, Jane Doe may do the following:

- Try to decipher what she feels you would do if you were conscious. This kind of guidance is often called "substituted judgment." A Jane Doe trying to use substituted judgment might try, for example, to recall conversations she's had with you on the subject of the kind of medical care or choices being offered. She may know that your religion forbids you to take a certain class of drugs and that you would prefer a riskier course of treatment rather than consume a drug against your religious principles.
- Try to do what she feels is in your best interests. The so-called "best interests" model of decision making would have Jane decide, as objectively as she could, what course of treatment you *should* receive. Let's say you are in a coma and you've developed pneumonia. The drug the doctors would like to use to treat the pneumonia is forbidden by Jane's and your religious beliefs. Jane knows that if you were unconscious you would rather risk death than inject the forbidden drug. And

Jane herself would rather risk death than inject the drug were she lying unconscious. Nevertheless, Jane authorizes the doctors to administer the drug to you under the theory that increasing your chance of staying alive physically is what's in your best interests—from the viewpoint of a reasonable and objective person.

- Simply follow her own judgment. Jane Doe may use her own judgment without trying to be objective at all. This is the so-called "subjective" model of decision making. It wouldn't matter what a panel of medical authorities thought was in your best interests. The only thing that would matter is what Jane Doe alone, using her own subjective judgments and opinions, wanted.

Because merely appointing Jane Doe, without saying more, leaves unclear what guidance, standards, or sources she should use to come to a decision about what doctors can do for and to you, you should always consider clarifying what that guidance should be: substituted judgment, best interests/objective, or subjective.

If you trust Jane's thinking on emergency medical matters, you may be comfortable with a subjective standard. If not, even if you trust her implicitly, you should strongly consider a best interests/objective standard. The substituted judgment standard is best for circumstances where you have made your wishes clear in an almost comprehensive way to Jane Doe. Otherwise, she will have no guidance for making her decisions in the moment of crisis.

Here are some examples of language you may use that reflects each of the three standards. Notice that none of the language tells Jane specifically what she should do, because the specific treatment will never be known beforehand.

BEST INTERESTS TEST

"I hereby appoint Jane Doe as my medical proxy, having all powers as I would have were I conscious, to make all decisions affecting my health, including decisions having the risk of death. In making her decision, Jane is to be guided by what she views as in my best medical interests. My best medical interests are to be determined without regard to contrary religious belief. Jane may, but shall not be required, to consult with one or more physicians to make this determination."

SUBSTITUTED JUDGMENT

"I hereby appoint Jane Doe as my medical proxy, having all powers as I would have were I conscious, to make all decisions affecting my health, including decisions having the risk of death. In making her decision, Jane is to be guided by what she feels I would wish to have done were I still conscious and able to make the decision. Any opinions I have concerning the treatments or courses of actions being considered shall theretofore be given greatest weight, with written opinions holding greater weight than oral ones. Jane's recollections of my views should take precedence over any other person's recollections of my orally expressed opinions."

SUBJECTIVE TEST

"I hereby appoint Jane Doe as my medical proxy, having all powers as I would have were I conscious, to make all decisions affecting my health, including decisions having the risk of death. In making her decision, Jane is to be guided by her own judgment, and that judgment shall be given sole weight, notwithstanding contrary opinions of any others including medical professionals, religious professionals, or others. Neither shall any recollections of any opinions I may have expressed, either expressed orally or in writing, take precedence over Jane's opinion, which shall be conclusive and binding.

BEYOND MERELY DESIGNATING A PROXY

The second broad category of advance directives goes beyond merely designating Jane Doe as a proxy. These advance directives try to establish what decisions should be made under which circumstances. For example, an advance directive of this type might say:

"I hereby designate Jane Doe as my medical proxy to act on my behalf in circumstances where I am unconscious and in need of medical care. In such circumstances, if brain damage has been sustained, I authorize Jane Doe to consent to any medical procedure that would give me a better than 50 percent chance of surviving with my cognitive reasoning abilities intact, even if such procedure endangers my ability to survive. In all circumstances not involving brain damage (but involving more than a 50 percent chance that I may die), Jane Doe's judgment shall be conclusive, regardless of opinions I may have expressed or opinions of medical doctors, or religious doctrine."

Advance directives can also direct that special medical procedures be taken to save your life if you are unconscious. This special type of advance directive would, in effect, be a living will.

Because advance directives are powerful documents, many states will not recognize an individual as your medical proxy unless the advance directive has been executed under circumstances that tend to minimize the risk of fraud. Various kinds of formalities are required to reduce this risk. For example, some states require that advance directives always be written, notarized, and witnessed by at least two persons other than the medical proxy. Although these rather rigid requirements help to reduce the risk of fraud, many times people don't make an advance directive until they're about to go into surgery, and they're unlikely to want to go through the tedious steps of notarization and assembling witnesses.

At the other end of the spectrum is the Uniform Health Care Decisions Act drafted by the Uniform Law Commissioners in 1995. Because the Uniform Law Commissioners is not a legislature, its "laws" do not have the force of law until they are adopted by the legislature of each individual state. So far, only two states, Maine and New Mexico, have adopted the Uniform Health Care Decision Act, and each made changes to the Uniform Act before adopting it.

The most significant achievement of the Uniform Act is that it brings into one place concepts of advance directives, living wills, and even organ donation. The most controversial part of the Uniform Act is that it recognizes oral advance directives, dispensing entirely with requirements of notarization, witnessing, and writing. The Uniform Act gives priority to decisions made by orally designated proxies if no written directive has been made. The Act recognizes that in most circumstances proxies are the persons designated by a patient to his or her doctor and requires the doctor to enter the designation in the patient's medical chart.

New Mexico's version of the Uniform Act eliminates the provisions on organ and tissue donation and also permits a "domestic partner" to make health care decisions for a patient who has not made any other designation. New Mexico also requires that at least two health care professionals concur that the patient is incapable of making medical decisions before a proxy can be recognized.

Appendix

RESOURCES AND ORGANIZATIONS

Addresses and telephone numbers are provided to help you care for your elderly relative.

ADAPTIVE DEVICES
ABLEDATA (assistive devices)
8455 Colesville Rd.
Silver Spring, MD 20910
800-346-2742

Adaptive Device
Locator System
Academic Software
331 W. Second St.
Lexington, KY 40507
606-233-2332

ALZHEIMER'S DISEASE
Alzheimer's Association
919 N. Michigan Ave.
Suite 1000
Chicago, IL 60611
800-272-3900

Alzheimer's Disease Education and Referral Center
P.O. Box 8250
Silver Spring, MD 20907
800-438-4380

National Institute of Neurological Disorders and Stroke
Information Office
Building 31, Room 8A16
31 Center Dr., MSC2540
Bethesda, MD 20892
800-352-9424

CAREGIVER SERVICES
Aging Network Services
4400 East West Highway
Suite 907
Bethesda, MD 20814
301-657-4329

Children of Aging Parents
1609 Woodbourne Rd.
Suite 302A
Levittown, PA 19057
215-945-6900
800-227-7294

National Family Caregivers Association
9621 East Bexhill Drive
Kensington, MD 20895-3104
301-942-6430
301-942-2302 (fax)
800-896-3650

145

DRIVING SAFETY
AAA Foundation For Traffic Safety
1440 New York Ave., NW, Suite 201
Washington, DC 20005
800-305-7233
202-638-5944

National Safety Council
1121 Spring Lake Dr.
Itasca, IL 60143
800-621-6244

FINANCES
American Institute of Certified
Public Accountants
1211 Avenue of the Americas
New York, NY 10036
212-596-6200
800-862-4272

American Society of CLU & CFC
(Chartered Life Underwriters
and Chartered Financial Consultants)
270 South Bryn Mawr Ave.
Bryn Mawr, PA 19010
800-392-6900

Certified Financial Planner
Board of Standards
1660 Lincoln St., Suite 3050
Denver, CO 80264
303-830-7543

International Association for Financial
Planning
Two Concourse Parkway, Suite 800
Atlanta, GA 30328
800-945-4237
404-395-1605

National Association of Personal
Financial Advisors
1130 Lake Cook Rd., Suite 105
Buffalo Grove, IL 60089
800-366-2732

National Association of Securities
Dealers
9513 Key West Ave.
Rockville, MD 20850
800-289-9999

National Foundation for Consumer
Credit
8611 Second Ave., Suite 100
Silver Spring, MD 20910
800-388-2227

Pension Rights Center
918 16th St., NW, Suite 704
Washington, DC 20006
202-296-3776

Medicare Hotline
800-638-6833

GENERAL
American Association of Retired
Persons (AARP)
601 E St., NW
Washington, DC 20049
202-434-2277
800-424-3410

American Occupational Therapy
Association
P.O. Box 31220
4720 Montgomery Dr.
Bethesda, MD 20824
301-652-2682

Consumer Information Center
"Catalogue"
Pueblo, CO 81009
719-948-3334

Elder Care Locator
800-677-1116

Elderhostel
P.O. Box 1959
Wakefield, MA 01880
617-426-7788

National Association for Hispanic
Elderly
3325 Wilshire Blvd.
Los Angeles, CA 90010
213-487-1922

National Association of Professional
Geriatric Care Managers
1604 North Country Club Rd.
Tucson, AZ 85716
520-881-8008

National Association of Social Workers
750 First St., NE
Washington, DC 20002
800-638-8799 (ext. 291)

National Caucus and Center on Black
Aged
1424 K St., NW, Suite 500
Washington, DC 20005
202-637-8400

National Federation of Interfaith
Volunteer Caregivers
368 Broadway, Suite 103
Kingston, NY 12401
914-331-1358
800-350-7438

Older Women's League
666 11th St., NW, Suite 700
Washington, DC 20001
800-825-3695

Social Security Administration
800-772-1213

Well Spouse Foundation
P.O. Box 801
New York, NY 10023
212-644-1241
800-838-0879

HEALTH
Better Hearing Institute
Hearing Helpline
P.O. Box 1840
Washington, DC 20012
800-327-9355

Cancer Information Service
National Cancer Institute
Building 31, Room 10A24
Bethesda, MD 20892
800-422-6237

Hearing Aid Helpline
20361 Middlebelt Rd.
Livonia, MI 48152
800-521-5247

National Association for Home Care
519 C St., NE
Washington, DC 20002
202-547-7424

Visiting Nurse Associations of America
3801 East Florida Ave., Suite 900
Denver, CO 80210
800-426-2547

HOSPICE
Choice in Dying
200 Varick Street
New York, NY 10014
212-366-5540

Foundation for Hospice and Home
Care
320 A St., NE
Washington, DC 20002
202-547-6586

Hospice Association of America
519 C St., NE
Washington, DC 20002
202-546-4759

Hospice Helpline
National Hospice Organization
1901 N. Moore St., Suite 901
Arlington, VA 22209
800-658-8898

National Hospice Organization
1901 N. Moore Street
Suite 901
Arlington, VA 22209
703-243-5900
800-658-8898

HOUSING
AARP Home Equity
Information Center
601 East St., NW
Washington, DC 20049
202-434-2277

American Association of Homes and
Services for the Aging
901 East St., NW, Suite 500
Washington, DC 20004
202-783-2242

Assisted Living Facilities
Association of America
9411 Lee Highway
Plaza Suite J
Fairfax, VA 22031
703-691-8100

Continuing Care Accreditation
Commission
901 East St., NW, Suite 500
Washington, DC 20004-2037
202-783-2242

National Center for Home Equity
Conversion
7373 147th St., Suite 115
Apple Valley, MN 55124

National Shared Housing
Resource Center
321 East 25th St.
Baltimore, MD 21218
410-235-4454

INSURANCE
Center for Medicare Advocacy
P.O. Box 350
Willimantic, CT 06226
203-456-7790
800-262-4414

Medicare Hotline
800-638-6833
800-492-6603 in Maryland

National Association of Claims
Assistance Professionals
5329 South Main St.
Downers Grove, IL 60515
800-660-0665

National Consumers League
1710 K St., NW
Washington, DC 20006
202-835-3323

National Insurance
Consumer Helpline
1025 Connecticut Ave., NW
Suite 1200
Washington, DC 20036
800-942-4242

United Seniors Health Cooperative
1331 H St., NW, Suite 500
Washington, DC 20005
202-393-6222

LEGAL ASSISTANCE
American Bar Association
750 North Lake Shore Drive
Chicago, IL 60611
312-988-5000
800-964-4253

Commission on Legal Problems of the Elderly
American Bar Association
1800 M St., NW, South Lobby
Washington, DC 20036
202-662-8690

Legal Counsel for the Elderly
American Association of Retired Persons
601 E St., NW
Washington, DC 20049
800-424-3410

National Academy of Elder
Law Attorneys
1604 North Country Club Road
Tucson, AZ 85716
602-881-4005

MEAL SERVICES/NUTRITION
National Association of Meal Programs
101 North Alfred St., Suite 202
Alexandria, VA 22314
703-548-5558

National Meals on Wheels Foundation
2675 44th St., SW, Suite 305
Grand Rapids, MI 49509
800-999-6262

Nutrition Hotline
American Dietetic Association
216 West Jackson Blvd., Suite 800
Chicago, IL 60606
800-366-1655

MENTAL HEALTH
SERVICES/SUPPORT
American Association for Marriage and Family Therapy
1100 17th St., NW, 10th Floor
Washington, DC 20036
800-374-2638

American Psychiatric Association
1400 K St., NW
Washington, DC 20005
202-682-6220

American Psychological Association
750 First St., NE
Washington, DC 20002
800-374-2721

American Self-Help Clearinghouse
25 Pocono Rd.
St. Clares-Riverside Medical Center
Denville, NJ 07834
201-625-7101

National Alliance for the Mentally Ill
2102 Wilson Blvd., Suite 302
Arlington, VA 22201
800-950-6294

National Association of Social Workers
750 First St., NE
Washington, DC 20002
202-408-8600

National Foundation for Depressive Illness
P.O. Box 2257
New York, NY 10116
800-248-4381

National Institute of Mental Health
Public Inquiries Office
Room 7C-02
5600 Fishers Lane
Rockville, MD 20857

National Self-Help Clearinghouse
25 West 43rd St., Room 620
New York, NY 10036
212-354-8525

NURSING HOMES

Concerned Relatives of Nursing Home
Patients
P.O. Box 18820
Cleveland Heights, OH 44118
216-321-0403

National Citizens' Coalition for
Nursing Home Reform
1424 16th St., NW, Suite 202
Washington, DC 20036
202-332-2275

Nursing Home Information Service
National Council of Senior Citizens
1331 F St., NW
Washington, DC 20004
202-347-8800 ext. 340/341

CANADIAN AGENCIES AND PRIVATE SERVICES

Canadian Association of Retired
Persons (CARP)
CARP is a national advocacy
organization for Canadians over 50,
with 335,000 members.
CARP may be reached by e-mail at
info@fifty-plus.net

Community Care for the Elderly
and Disabled
Social Planning Department
Duke Tower, Scotia Square
P.O. Box 1749
Halifax, NS B3J 3A5
(902) 421-6420 (phone)
(902) 421-6400 (fax)

The Don Mills Foundation for Senior
Cititzens
1 Overland Drive
North York, Ontario M3C2C3
(416) 447-7244 (phone)
(416) 447-6364 (fax)
e-mail: dmfseniors.org/main.htm/

Langley Home Support Service
22424 Fraser Highway
Langley, B.C. V3A8N3
(604) 534-2581 (phone)
(604) 534-4099 (fax)
e-mail: lhss@uniserve.com

Mennonites in Canada
c/o Canadian Mennonite Health
Assembly
(510) 653-5719
The Mennonites operate
approximately 50 seniors' residences
or care homes in Canada, servicing
4,000 to 5,000 seniors. The first such
home was opened in 1921.

REFERENCES

Becker, P.M. and H.J. Cohen 1984. The functional approach to the care of the elderly: A conceptual framework. J. of the American Geriatrics Society 32: 923–29

Blazer, D. "Evaluating the Family of the Elderly Patient in *A Family Approach to Health Care of the Elderly*. Edited by Blazer, D. and Siegler, J. 13–32 Menlo Pk, CA: Addison-Wesley 1984

Burger, S.G., Virginia Fraser, Sara Hunt, Barbara Frank and The National Citizens' Coalition for Nursing Home Reform *Nursing Homes* American Source Books/Impact Publsihers, Inc. CA 1996

Darnell, J.C., et al. 1986 Medication use by ambulatory elderly: An in-home survey. J. of the American Geriatrics Society 34: 1–4

Edye, D., and Rich, J. *Psychological Distress in Aging: a Family Management Model*. Rockville, MD: Aspen Publications 1983

Greenberg, Vivian E. *Your Best is Good Enough: Aging Parents and Your Emotions*. Lexington Books NY 1989

Gruetzner, Howard. *Alzheimer's—A Caregiver's Guide and Source Book*. John Wiley & Sons, Inc. 1992

Haynes, R.B., D.L. Sackett & D.W. Taylor 1989. How to detect and manage low patient compliance in chronic illness. *Geriatrics* 355: 1–4

Hooyman, Nancy R. and Wendy Lustbader. *Taking Care of Your Aging Family Members*. A Practical Guide. The Free Press, A Division of MacMillan, Inc. NY 1986

Inlander, Charles B., Michael A. Donn and J. Lynne Dodson, *Lont-Term Care and Its Alternatives*. People's Medical Society 1996

Kalb, Claudia. Focus on Your Health: "Caring from Afar." Newsweek 9/22/97

Kenny, James, Ph.D. and Stephen Spicer, M.D. *Elder Care*. Prometheus Books NY 1989

Klein, L.E., P.S. German & D.M. Levine 1981. Adverse drug reaction's among the elderly: A reassessment. J. of the American Geriatrics Society 29: 525–30

Kouri, Mary K. Ph.D. *Keys to Survival for Caregivers*. 1992 Barron's Educational Series, Inc.

Levin, Nora Jean *How to Care for Your Parents*. W.W. Norton and Co. NY 1997

Lipton, Ph.D., Helene Levens and Philip R. Lee, M.D. with contributions by Mark S. Freeland, Ph.D. *Drugs and the Elderly*. Stanford Univ. Press: Stanford, CA 1988

Morris, Virginia *How to Care for Aging Parents*. Workman Publishing Co., Inc. NY 1996

Munley, Anne. *The Hospice Alternative*. A new Context for Death and Dying. Basic Gooks, Inc. NY 1983

Sobel, K.G., and G.M. McCart 1983. Drug use and accidental falls in an intermediate case facility. *Drug Intelligence & Clinical Pharmacy* 17: 539–42

Zimmerman, M.D., F.A.C.S. *Hospice: Complete Care for the Terminally Ill*. Urban and Schwarzenberg, Germany 1981

Index

f indicates figure; t indicates table

A

Abilities assessment:
checklist, 20–21
goals of, 22
overview of, 19
Adaptations, for home care:
funding for, 108
resources and organizations for, 145
types of, 107–108
Adult day-care:
benefits of, 117
evaluation of, 117
Medicaid coverage of, 118
pre-participation examination of
relative, 118–119
standards for, 118
transportation for, 117
Advance directives:
definition of, 139
fraud considerations, 143
living wills and, differences
between, 139
medical proxies
description of, 139–140
guidance standards
best interests, 140–142
subjective, 141–142
substituted judgment, 140, 142
methods of providing, 139
oral types of, 143
Uniform Health Care Decisions Act,
143–144
Alzheimer's disease. *See also* Dementia
resources and organizations for, 145

American Association of Retired
Persons (AARP):
address of, 148
description of, 3, 7
long-term care policies offered by,
129–130
Apartments, 103t
"Asset dumping," for Medicaid
coverage qualification, 125
Assisted living residences. *See also*
Housing
activities in, 86
amenities of, 86
costs per day, 86
description of, 23, 85–86
goals of, 86
licensing of, 85
living arrangements of, 85–86
staffing of, 86
transfer to another facility, 86
Avoiders, 12

B

Bathing:
considerations for, 35
skills necessary for, 20
Bathroom, safety considerations for, 32
Bedroom, safety considerations for, 32
Behavior changes:
in elders with dementia, 51–54
physical problems and, relationship
between, 54
Best interests standard, of medical
proxies, 140–142

NOTES

NOTES

NOTES

NOTES

2